08807

WAKE UP, CANADA!

Reflections on Vital National Issues

C.W. Peterson

EDITED AND WITH AN INTRODUCTION BY
DAVID C. JONES

Abridged Edition

THE UNIVERSITY OF ALBERTA PRESS

This abridged edition published by
The University of Alberta Press
Athabasca Hall
Edmonton, Alberta
Canada   T6G 2E8

This abridged edition copyright © The University of Alberta Press 1989

ISBN 0-88864-203-2

Canadian Cataloguing in Publication Data
Peterson, C. W. (Charles Walter), 1868–1944.
  Wake up, Canada!

  Originally published: Toronto : Macmillan, 1919.
  ISBN 0-88864-203-2

  1. Canada - Politics and government - 1911–1921.*
2. Canada - Economic conditions - 1867–1918.* I. Jones,
David C., 1943- II. Title.
FC555.P48 1989   971.061   C89-091223-8
F1034.P48 1989

Cover illustration: NA 1451-16, Glenbow.

Typesetting by The Typeworks, Vancouver, British Columbia

Printed by Gagne Printing Ltd., Louiseville, Quebec, Canada

Contents

EDITOR'S COMMENT

Wake Up, Canada! is a superb reflection of Canadian dreams and obsessions at the end of the Great War. In this abridgement I sought to preserve the reflection and the abiding issues. I hoped to enhance the sharpness of the work, ease its readability, and speed its pace, without losing substance. My model was Peterson's own editorials in the *Farm and Ranch Review* which were tighter, more focused and less discursive than his book. I wished to show Peterson in all lights, and I allowed him repetition for effect. Yet, despite how revealing the volume was, it needed cutting to eliminate unnecessary duplication; certain gratuitous, innocuous statements or platitudes; preliminary thought and afterthought, beside-the-point introductions and other segments lacking unity; the odd, meandering, listless discussion; and idle speculation based on unconfirmed news despatches received the day he was writing, or on what foreign governments seem to have been intending. I also slashed the discussion of agricultural taxation in Britain, industrial expenditures in Russia, and Confucian schools in China. The overall effect, I trust, is that the motherload of matters central to an era is exposed to the modern reader in all its richness, complexity and allure.

Acknowledgements

I thank the Western Canada Publications Project for its commitment to our literary heritage. For their counsel and other support, I identify David Hall, Brian Titley, John Foster, Paul Voisey and David Barregar. For permission to reprint the manuscript, I note Mrs. Else Peterson. The Chinook Country Chapter of the Alberta Historical Society graciously allowed me to build the introduction on my "Ruminations of a Rustic—C.W. Peterson," in Max Foran and Sheilagh Jameson's *Citymakers—Calgarians after the Frontier* (1987). The Social Sciences and Humanities Research Council of Canada and the University of Calgary Research Grants Committee kindly funded the research, and the Alberta Foundation for the Literary Arts, the publication.

C. W. Peterson in 1938 at age 70, six years before his death. NA 4945-1, Glenbow.

INTRODUCTION

David C. Jones

The Best Informed Man on Western Conditions

When Charles W. Peterson, the esteemed dean of Canada's agrarian editors, died in Calgary in February 1944, former Prime Minister Arthur Meighen confessed frankly—"He was in my judgement, the best informed man on Western conditions and the soundest thinker on Western conditions that we had in all Canada."[1] Many things made Peterson appealing to certain politicians, but perhaps the greatest was the fact that he never expected much from them. As he told a convention of lumbermen twenty years earlier, "We persist in regarding our problems as political when as a matter of fact they are economic and not susceptible to solution at the hands of government."[2] It was a sentiment that would have appealed to Meighen.

Far seeing, intensely logical, and with a mind for economic riddles, Peterson once said that he had spent his "whole life in spreading propaganda in favour of a clearer understanding of the dominant position of agriculture in the general scheme of life." After years of such toil, he admitted, "I am more and more impressed by what Louisburg has facetiously termed 'the infinite capacity of the human brain to withstand the introduction of knowledge.'"[3]

Born in Copenhagen in 1868, the son of an army officer, Charles Peterson was educated in an agricultural school in Denmark before emigrating to Great Britain for a year and then to Manitoba in

1888. After failing in his first farming venture south of Winnipeg, he promptly became an assistant general immigration agent for the Dominion and then spent four years in the Dominion Land Office in Calgary. In 1897 he was called to Regina to be deputy commissioner of agriculture for the North West Territories. After implanting the basic legislation the new provinces of Alberta and Saskatchewan would inherit, he returned to Calgary in 1902. In 1905, with M.D. Geddes, Peterson founded the *Farm and Ranch Review*. The next year he became general manager of the CPR Irrigation and Colonization Company, and in 1910 he was made superintendent of irrigation for the CPR. After retiring from the CPR, he returned to his first love, the *Review*. During the Great War, he was called to Ottawa to be secretary of the National Service Board and later deputy fuel controller of Canada. Following the war, he returned to the editorial chair he occupied until his death.[4]

Peterson's personality was deeply etched in his books, *Wake Up, Canada!* (1919), *The Fruits of the Earth* (1928), *Wheat—The Riddle of Markets* (1930), dozens of editorials and speeches, and the memories of those he knew. It was also imprinted in his handwriting. The most radical of my attempts to uncover his basic make-up involved the submission of two pages of Peterson's handwriting, plus a signature, to professional grapho-analyst W. David Barregar. Peterson's identity was not revealed to Barregar until after he submitted his report.

Grapho-analysis has long been the subject of legitimate, intensive research and requires formalized study of some years. It is based on the assumption that handwriting is a reflection of one's innate thinking processes, in fact, of one's very nature. As one scholar wrote:

handwriting, basically to be understood as a sum of crystallized gestures (micro-gestures), represents a many-sided index of underlying expressive impulses due to the central nervous system. The form of the letters, their relative size, the manner of connecting them, the slope of the script, the slant of the lines, pressure of pen, division of space, these and many other details, never identi-

Peterson at age 19 near the time of his abortive farming venture in Manitoba. NA 4945-3, Glenbow.

An afternoon tea at the residence of W.H. Hogg, manager of the Bank of Montreal, Regina, when C.W. was deputy commissioner of agriculture in the Territorial Government, 1899. Peterson standing second from right above his first wife Nel, Frederick Haultain standing on left. NA 1702-10, Glenbow.

cal in two different original scripts, are, in short, classification, criteria of the writer's taste, sense of space, temperament, clearness of thinking, etc. . . . [5]

Barregar concluded that Peterson was an independent thinker with an investigative mind who came to the point quickly and who relished detail. "He did not take things lying down. . . . He saw connections and had the ability to. . . sense things before others even suspected them," said Barregar. There was an urgency to his tasks, and he could push very hard, especially if he felt he was right. He could be domineering, with the odd flashes of temper, and he likely "would not have made a good 'obedient' employee." At the same time, as leader, he could sense the needs of others and easily establish rapport. Intriguingly, Barregar recorded that although Peterson was exceedingly capable, "he did not fully challenge his abilities."

While the process of deriving psychological and emotional characteristics from writing sometimes seems illogical, other times it appears quite sensible. To graphologists the entrance stroke into words reveals the way a writer approaches problems. In Peterson's case, the first letter almost always began immediately, with no flourishes or adornment—a clear mark of a man who was blunt and to the point, who seldom beat around the bush or flowered matters. The dotting of "i"'s, the placement of periods and the crossing of "t"'s can all indicate a writer's attention to detail. In Peterson's case, all were precisely placed, and the dots were rounded. Combined with the considerable speed with which he wrote, these factors indicate an acute focus on detail, an orderly and precise mind. The structure of the small "t," graphologists believe, is immensely revealing. The downstroke on Peterson's crossing suggested a dominant nature, and the cross in his signature flying to the right implied temper. Even the placement of the cross had meaning, and in Peterson's writing, Barregar was surprised to see it so low, given Peterson's other traits. The inference is that he may not have realized his full potential.

It took Barregar roughly two hours to compose this sketch; yet it is almost precisely the view I saw after a year of study of the sub-

The lovely Else Peterson, third wife of C.W., for whom he was eternally grateful. The book *The Fruits of the Earth* (1928) he dedicated to her "whose bright, intelligent comradeship and gentle forbearance is retarding the flight of time itself and radiantly illuminating the eventide of my life. . . ." NA 4945-2, Glenbow.

stance of Peterson's writing. Before commissioning the analysis, I had even concluded that this imposing figure might have been even more significant, given his obvious powers and sway.[6]

Peterson was married three times and had four children. His first wife, "Nel," died of heart trouble compounded by tuberculosis in 1906, the second, "Queenie," died of cancer in 1924. Shortly thereafter he met Else in Denmark, and they were married in 1926. By Else's reckoning, she was the last and "the best."

Peterson was president of the *Farm and Ranch Review* and the Western Printing and Lithographing and Hicks Engraving firms. He also had an interest in the Bassano Farming Company and the Crowfoot Farming Company, concerns embracing several thousand acres. A patrician farmer, he was backed by the considerable capital of associate H.H. Honens.

The Petersons and friends at a party at the William Pearce estate, 1930c. C.W. centre of top row with drink, Else in two-tone cloche hat and with fur collar, seated directly below. NA 4945-6, Glenbow.

C.W. as caddy, with Else and a friend, Banff, 1930s. NA 4945-7, Glenbow.

Peterson often travelled across the continent and overseas on trips that mixed business with pleasure. He liked theatre, museums and art, and he loved opera. In the early days he was friends with Colonel Dennis of the CPR, and at least once they did Gilbert and Sullivan together. He was a great reader and gardener. He neither hunted nor fished, nor enjoyed sports particularly, though he did condescend to be Else's caddy on occasion. A gourmand, he loved good food, avoided fats and rarely overate. He fancied ocean liners, luxurious appointments and fine living. A highlight of his social life was the small dinner parties and bridge games, Saturday nights, at which Peterson, called "Pete" or sometimes "C.W." by his friends, could be an exceedingly gracious host. Family friends were the Eric Harvies, the J.B. Corbetts, Harry Nolans, Austin de B Winters, the Harold Carsons, and several others mostly of the business community.[7]

Peterson was not given to much frivolity. Indeed, Eric McGreer, his office manager from 1929 to 1940, could not "remember any humor injected into anything in any way, shape or form." Once during a dinner party C.W. was dilating on a favorite topic, Danish agriculture, and he began to talk of greenhouses and then growing bananas in northern Europe—at which point McGreer burst into laughter! C.W. glared at him and snapped, "What are you laughing at?"[8]

The reaction seemed to capture Peterson's response to most things as he surveyed the world from his editorial chair. Very rarely were there jokes in his long columns, and even copies of his speeches which were usually written out in full on hand-sized memo paper never hinted of the content of the one or two "stories" inserted along the way. Generally he was much too serious to be funny. His obsession with the dismal science of economics and its application to the tragedy of agriculture throughout the interwar period did not dispose him to dwell on the lighter side of life for very long.

Nonetheless, he still displayed elements of humor. The conflicting demands of his broad readership (some 80,000 by 1930) struck him as comical, though perhaps more absurd. One day in 1927 the

first letter he opened thanked him for his loyal support of the
Wheat Pool; a second missive requested that he drop all wheat pool
propaganda entirely. A third expressed gratitude for the religious
column in the *Review,* and a fourth snorted that the *Review* was being turned into a Sunday School paper and ordered immediate can-
cellation![9] A few years later, he published more reactions:

"I am glad to note that you are beginning to see the light and oc-
casionally criticise your capitalistic friends," said one reader.

"Your hidebound admiration and support of the present economic system makes me sick..." said another.

"... I regret your present tendency to play into the hands of the
radical element, who seem bound to destroy what wiser generations have labouriously built up," said a third.[10]

The Divine Purpose of Armageddon

Peterson's *Wake Up, Canada!* was one of those remarkable pieces
that capture the ethos of an era. It was an attempt to draw meaning
from the ghastly sacrifices of the Great War and to revamp the
world accordingly. Superficially, the conflict was a struggle for
democracy; more profoundly, it was a *trial* of democracy. A
glorious ideal, it was in reality found wanting, a maladjustment certainly, and eminently remediable to the hardened, confident mind
of the victors of Armageddon.

The nature of the maladjustment Peterson soon clarified. Canada suffered from sharp divisions between East and West, capital
and labor, anglophones and francophones, urbanites and ruralites.
Fueling the discontent were two flammables—the first, mountain-
ous debt of the war and the national railways fiasco; the second, the
feeling of domination by forces malignant, a system inherently unfair, typified by machine politics, hidden agendas, and patronage by
the bushel.

Returned in Due Course

A pig belonging to an old lady called Mary, was stolen. So Mary went over to her neighbors making enquiries, and was told that Pat O'Donnel was the culprit. Mary then went to the priest and told him that Pat O'Donnel had her pig. The next time Pat went to confession, he said nothing about the pig. "Pat," said the priest, "are those all the sins you have committed?"

"Yes," answered Pat.

"Did you take Mary's pig, Pat?" asked the priest.

"Yes," answered Pat, "I did."

"Well," said the priest, "isn't that a sin?"

Pat stood silent for a minute, and the priest continued:

"There's a certain day coming when you'll have to say why you did this sin. I'll be there, you'll be there, Mary will be there, and the pig will be there. What will you say then?"

Pat again stood silent, and then replied: "I'll say, 'Here's your pig, Mary!'"

SOURCE: "Wit of the World," *Farm and Ranch Review,* April 4, 1920, p. 63.

A Triumph

As Pat boarded the train and took a seat there was a smile of triumph upon his face.

"What's the matter with you?" asked his friend.

Pat's countenance beamed satisfaction.

"Shure, I've been riding on this road for tin years an' I've got the best o' the company for once in me loife!"

"How's that?"

"I've just bought myself a return ticket, an'," lowering his voice to a whisper, "be-jabbers, I ain't coming back!"

SOURCE: "Wit of the World," *Farm and Ranch Review,* May 5, 1921, p. 39.

Beginning in 1918, the *Farm and Ranch Review* carried a "Wit of the World" column, comprised of light humor submitted by readers. For years prizes were awarded for the best submissions each issue—$1 for first, 50¢ for second (later 75¢ for second and 50¢ for third). In preparation of the journal, however, Peterson focused most of his energy on superb editorials.

Peterson cast the broad questions—how to inject a sense of citizenship, national identity, and original thinking in governance; how to stem the excessive demands of labor, the expanding ignorance of rural life, and the flood of one-dimensional lawyers swamping the legislatures; how to react to Bolshevism, the banking system, and state take-over of industry; how to rationalize taxes and tariffs to generate needed revenues without hamstringing national development; and how to discredit the false worship of the golden calf which equated wealth with happiness, thinkers and artists with drudges.

Throughout, Peterson confronted these challenges with a strange brew of biases. At heart he was a conservative influenced sporadically by the social message of the time, a conservative suspicious of the East, barristers, and banks, a pro-farmer with reservations about farm leadership and the single tax, an anti-socialist with a desire for better distribution of wealth, including inheritance taxes.

From time to time in Peterson's polemic the seeds of inconsistency sprouted. Regarding labor, he allowed that shorter hours and better pay achieved by industry were "excellent reforms"; but the thrust was misdirected because most of the palaver about more holidays and shorter hours was "founded upon absolutely wrong premises," inferring that "any sort of useful occupation is a necessary evil and that happiness only lies in idleness...." He claimed that "few worth-while social readjustments have been attained solely through moral suasion" and that labor would have gotten nowhere without "militant methods." But these methods were now abhorrent and out of touch with the "New Spirit."[11]

French Canadians Peterson patronized to death in a dizzying series of accusations and accolades. "Jean Baptiste," he asserted, "is not a fighting man, [and] the French press went into hysterics" at the thought of conscription, but Jean "cheerfully went to the front," unless he secured an exemption which he "seldom failed to do"! Quebec's contribution to the victory was not conspicuous, but its units "covered themselves in glory." Jean lived in the sixteenth century with Quebec "his country" and le cure his "deputy god"; Great Britain and France meant "no more to him than Nova Scotia or Saskatchewan—and that [was] nothing at all." Desperately he needed a speck of citizenship, yet there was "no better raw material anywhere." Certainly his church warranted Peterson's "deepest admiration, respect and regard," yet it was always insinuating itself "behind the throne." Sadly the French were forever dominating federal politics, yet the people were "a splendid race."[12] It was a case, plainly, of I love him, I love him not, but mostly I wonder about him.

On western issues Peterson was more convincing and more at home. *Wake Up, Canada!* fiercely critiqued the application of socialism to the country's ills, and at the end of a scenario, both pungent and futuristic, the "wage slaves" become "slaves without wages."[13] Similarly, the book demolished the much-vaunted single tax proposal, the age-old hoax of the infant industries argument, and the feather brained soldier settlement plans.

However impatient and importunate, the work was not pessimistic. Canada was "an Empire of boundless opportunities," said Peterson. Compared with its natural resources, "the wealth of the Indies fades into insignificance...."[14] Double the population and half the debt; treble it and forget the debt—that was his promise.

The Ensuing Tragedy

For Peterson the interwar period thus opened with great expectations. Like others, he was fed by the manna of triumph and rebirth generated by the conflict. In good company, he forecasted the resumption of the exuberant settlement period and the coming of an era of unprecedented prosperity. With several, he saw the annihilation of European cattle stocks and predicted that western Canadians would participate in the bonanza of replenishing some twenty million head of breeding stock.[15]

Hopes were dashed, however, as the demand never materialized, and meat consumption dropped off, abetted by a fad of vegetarianism. A phenomenal increase in American tariffs then absolutely prostrated the Canadian livestock industry. As exports fell off, freight rates, taxes and the cost of living escalated, and agricultural prices plummeted.

These maladies were less than half the story, for the interwar period featured the profoundest tragedy ever to afflict western agriculture. Interminable drought descended upon the dry belt beginning in 1917, and by 1926, after half a dozen commissions, half the Alberta southeast was abandoned. In the vast Tilley East region alone, 80 percent of the settlers left across an area of 1.5 million acres.[16] In the irrigated sections, a fortune had been poured out under the mistaken assumption that the mere construction of irrigation works would create irrigated agriculture. Initial plans had underestimated costs and settlers' ability to repay and to adapt to a new form of farming without credit facilities, proper ground leveling, or advice. After more investigations and more abandonments, Peterson concluded that the history of irrigation to 1937 had been, with a few exceptions, "a very doleful story of failure."[17]

Within this tragic context, Peterson spent the last twenty-five years of his life. Ever reflecting, assessing, struggling with the conundrum of markets, desperately tearing at the veil which obscured his vision, he moved through the forlorn era armed with a somewhat old-fangled conservative business ideology. A natural balancer of most antagonistic viewpoints, he considered himself constitutionally unfit for partisan politics. "Personally, I can't come anywhere near seeing eye to eye on all questions with a political party," he once wrote.[18] Drawing inspiration from his stint with the efficient non-party government of the Territories, he consistently held aloof from political entanglements, believing that it enhanced his stature as an independent critic. This position solidified with the flowering of the farmers' political movement and its proliferation of official organs which he believed, quite rightly, to be a megaphone of the party oligarchy and thus incapable of self-criticism. "The independent press," he concluded about his own paper, "must be the watch-dog and organ of the rank and file of farmers."[19]

As he played this role, Peterson witnessed much that displeased him. After the war, the reform effervescence boiled over, spewing out a spate of caustic carpers bent on overturning the old order.

Early officers of the *Farm and Ranch Review*—C.W. flanked by E.L. Richardson, left, and M.D. Geddes, right, 1922c. NA 1451-16, Glenbow.

These ameliorators were among the first to elicit comment from the argus-eyed Peterson.

Instinctively, Peterson distrusted demagogues and spellbinders who drew attention to every evil under the sun, urging a thousand renovations, all in the name of uplift, while never addressing the farmer's elemental problems which were economic. "Every crack-brained aberration, every silly obsession, every impudent social adventure, provided it receives the sanction of the new idealism," he wrote, "is hawked abroad with insistent eloquence or senseless clamor."[20] The farm movement had surely entered "The Age of Bunk." The world was infested with "a horde of wild-eyed reformers" and "enthusiastic nuts" bent on precipitating an avalanche of social legislation.[21] Pointing to the United Farmer Conventions which annually paraded before bewildered delegates what to him was a ridiculous succession of resolutions ranging from anti-cigarette legislation to changes in divorce laws and the abolition of titles in Canada,[22] he gleefully quoted an American agrarian journal:

> To these reformers the practical is unworthy of attention. To ig-nore completely the fundamental traits of human nature is the cardinal point of their doctrine. Societies for the relief of dis-tressed burglars, associations for the amelioration of the boredom of setting hens by hanging instructive pictures in the chickenhouse, inquiries into the possibility of intellectual devel-opment among fishes, devotion to the abstraction of speculation rather than to the actual problems of life—all of these are the symptoms of the mental shallowness and feebleness of mind which has come to be taken as a mark of intellectual distinction and superiority to the herd.[23]

Social reformers, Peterson believed, true to his conservative roots, stifled initiative and self-reliance: "They would insure us and equip us to cope with every evil and hardship that befalls man—free hospitals, free university education, unemployment and sickness in-surance, minimum wages, fixation of prices and all the rest of it." Such measures led to indolence, improvidence and irresponsibil-ity—to a society so mindless and spiritless that it could do nothing for itself.[24] Moreover, such reform to Peterson was diversionary; as he said, ". . . what in Sam Hill have all these issues got to do with agricultural business problems?"[25]

The sentiment brought C.W. into direct conflict with H.W. Wood, spiritual leader and president of the UFA. Peterson resisted the confrontation until August 1923 when frustration over the fail-ure to establish the Wheat Pool flared into an irascible attack on Wood. Several things about Wood irked Peterson—he was a social-ist mesmerizer who dabbled overmuch on uplift matters; he had an obtuse obsession with blaming "certain mysterious 'interests'" whenever anything went wrong; and he seemed versed in nothing economic, in particular in the great danger of overproduction. Peterson damned him as a man "of no outstanding business experience" who ran the UFA more like "a Sunday School convention than a business institution."[26]

Peterson paid for his temerity in excoriating the demigod Wood when *The UFA* magazine unleashed an acidic counter assault. Drawing attention to Peterson's insults and to his devout prayers for a miracle that the vast increases in world wheat acreage since 1914 would not result in overproduction, the paper mused, "Is it possible that Mr. Peterson's fervent prayers may have had something to do with the hail and rust damage in Western Canada this year, and that it may yet bring on a devastating frost in Alberta. Who knows? And was Mr. Peterson responsible for the lean years of drought, grasshopper plagues, etc.? If so, might it be suggested that he operate more generally, and less locally?"[27]

Then Wood himself lambasted Peterson for his "editorial stupidity" and his moral duplicity in advocating the pool while refusing to sign up his own companies. Peterson had claimed that most of the large farmers had "heavy and urgent financial obligations to meet and could not delay realization upon the crop" until the pool was operational. "I presume the logical interpretation of this is either that Mr. Peterson was urging the organization of the pool for the benefit of small farmers who have no obligations to meet, or that the obligations of the small farmer do not count... " said Wood. "Mr. Peterson's attitude toward the Wheat Pool seems to be, 'let George try it out and if it works all right I'll come in later.'"[28]

Peterson's explanation was that the crops of the Bassano Farming Company and the Crowfoot Farming Company "had been contracted for before there was any suggestion of a wheat pool," and that four-fifths of the crop had "already been threshed, shipped and delivered, and the balance [would] be on wheels, long before the pool is in a position to even begin operations."[29]

The spat subsided, and by Christmas Peterson was happy that a bountiful crop in many areas sold at higher prices than anticipated. "Mr. H.W. Wood was more nearly right in his prophetic utterances on the subject of the wheat market than the editor of the 'Review,'" he admitted, only partly convinced. "We will hope that there is somewhere in the human mind and heart a fixed idea that no matter how vast over-production may become, wheat will not go below a certain living price. . . . If there is—and one almost concludes there is—such a hidden instinct in us all, we are face to face with a new principle in economics."[30]

While the opposition between the two men never again reached the same intensity, Peterson nursed an abiding resentment toward Wood. After Wood was elected UFA President for the umpteenth time and was also named chairman of the Wheat Pool, Peterson reminded readers of Wood's still reverberating denunciation of interlocking directorates.[31]

Later in his distinctly unmemorable novel, *The Fruits of the Earth* (1928), Peterson invested half the characters, plus naturally the narrator, with his own viewpoint. In particular, C.W. was Dick Anstruther, the hero, who is elected a farmer MLA, and his father, who personifies wisdom and is called most aptly, "The Sage." Some of Dick's statements appear almost verbatim as Peterson editorials. Dick objects to the stress on the social reform question, "as if we were a Sunday School Convention." Later, someone says, "the old man," who is the idealistic but impractical Wood, "is nuts on up-lift." And the narrator adds, "he and his fantastic social reform hobbies constituted a grave menace to a sound and practical development of the agrarian political movement in Canada. At one point Peterson parodies a speech of the old man's: "Let us so perform our glorious task that generations to come may arise and call us blessed."[32]

Throughout, the wise Sage, like Peterson, follows world events closely, studies the results of experimental farms, promotes irrigation, and dilates on the evils of overproduction. In the end, Dick becomes minister of public works in the new government, a job C.W. may have coveted, given the egregious extravagance of former administrations on public buildings, a folly Peterson repeatedly scored.

Not surprisingly, Peterson opposed socialism which he believed was killing the farmers' movement by dissipating its energy and ascribing to the state responsibilities which rightfully belonged to the individual. During the Depression, he considered the upper leader-ship of the CCF "a joke," and he asserted that the brain trust of the party had "no use for the well-meaning but ranting and unpractical Woodsworth and Irvine."[33] "At the bottom of the socialist creed," he ruminated, "lies a heavy layer of unreasoning envy and hatred of those who have made a material success of life, even though it has almost invariably been earned by sole reason of hard work, in-telligence and early self-sacrifice and only in a few instances by luck." Peterson took pleasure in underscoring the conclusion of Clarence Darrow who, after years of devoted struggle to social reform, said—"It's no use. The underdog, poor thing, is the un-derdog because of what he is."[34]

Peterson never seriously attempted to distinguish between social-ism and communism; so his broadsides against left wing politics were meant for all species of the beast. It was his notion of efficient criticism. The problem with communism was that life was essen-tially competitive and that the wise and industrious always out-shone the dull and the listless. "A non-competitive social system with our present large percentage of selfish, lazy and irresponsible members of the community," Peterson intoned, "would of course be absolutely intolerable."[35] The subject so animated him during the Depression that he even printed comedian Eddie Cantor's joke that "a communist is a man who owns nothing and invites everybody to share it with him."[36]

Peterson held as little love for organized labor. Repeatedly he disputed claims of the advocates of farm-labor alliances that farmers were part laborers and part capitalists. To his thinking, at least by the mid-twenties, the two had absolutely nothing in com-mon. The farmer was a capitalist, pure and simple, and an em-ployer of labor.[37] The two were fundamentally contenders, and the best example of their opposition was the way railroad unions through ubiquitous strike threats exacted high wages which rebounded on the farmer in high freight rates, high tariffs to keep out cheaper produced foreign products, and higher costs of most goods.

For every dollar the average Canadian rail employee earned in

1914, he got $2.25 in 1923. In 1914 Canadians paid $2 for each mile of freight train moved; in 1923, they paid $4.90.[38] Across the continent, the gap between railway incomes and farm incomes struck Peterson as preposterous. In 1922, he quoted an American source to the effect that the engineer on a small branch line got $4400 a year, or more than the Governor of Tennessee, baggagemen got more than assistant professors, and flagmen and porters on another branch got more than district attorneys-general for the state. High school teachers were given $125–$147 a month while switchmen received $188.[39]

The effect of Canadian mine unions was similar. "I'm afraid, I cannot shed any tears over the state of the Bohunk miner in Alberta receiving $8.25 for an eight-hour day and now ready to go on strike again," he wrote in 1924. "Supposing I prostrated myself before this unemotional magnate and drew a harrowing word picture of the suffering and hardship of the unfortunate farmer in dry season, who cannot afford to buy coal at the luxury prices necessitated by the outrageous wages these pirates are insisting upon. Would it touch his heart? Not by a jugfull. He doesn't care a tinker's d--- about the state of the farmer."[40]

It was thus little wonder that Peterson considered farmer delegates visiting labor conventions to assure them of undying support a sham: "Great God, can monumental stupidity go farther than this? The suffering host extends greetings to the greedy parasite, inviting him to go on feasting sumptuously on his weakened body!"[41]

When the doctrine of Social Credit, as preached by Major Douglas, gained momentum in the thirties, Peterson ridiculed it. Douglas's mind, he believed, functioned according to the counsel of a great cynic—"*If you would make your doctrine immortal, make it incomprehensible, for then no one can prove that it is wrong.*"[42] Peterson's tirades grew so insistent and his commentaries so trenchant that the legal firm of Carlile and McCarthy implored him, unsuccessfully, to lead the opposition to the Socreds.[43] What annoyed the level-headed Peterson was that the Aberhart government was elected on the promise of ushering in a new economic order, and after fourteen months in office, it had done nothing and had never had a plan in mind at all.

The ignorance of legislators in Edmonton, coupled with the howling of dissident Socred backbenchers in 1937, transcended anything Peterson had witnessed since the birth of the West. "Legislation has been passed obviously beyond provincial jurisdiction, and promptly disallowed, class hatred has been fanned to white heat, families have been split. Decency has departed, venom has taken its place, and the whole tone of public life has been swept into the gutter," lamented Peterson. "Arbitrary powers have been taken to tax, license and control everyone and everything in the most barefaced autocratic and ruthless manner." Then turning to the young new minister of trade and industry, he hung Ernest Manning's hide out to dry—"The allwise superman who is going to be the dictator of Alberta business, with supreme power over everybody, employer and employee, is—the Good Lord save us all!—a conceited, half-baked youngster whose sole business experience has been gained as assistance preacher at the Aberhart Bible Institute. Alberta, in fact, has become the laughing stock of the wide world."[44]

All this Peterson claimed to have taken with equanimity, but when the beleaguered and bewildered government introduced the infamous press gag bill, he exploded. The bill proposed to muzzle the papers and extract costly advertising space free of charge so as to flood the province with Social Credit propaganda. Noting that the law had not yet received royal assent, Peterson pronounced, "If and when it does, I hereby serve notice on the legislative lunatic asylum in Edmonton, that, law or no law, they will turn the "Review" into a filthy, political propaganda sheet only over my dead body."[45]

An Aura of Gloom

These outpourings issued from a much deeper distress. The interwar period, climaxed by the Depression, brought Peterson, like so many others, to the wall. His business concerns teetered pre-

Farm and Ranch Review

VOLUME XXVII
NUMBER 9

5¢

CIRCULATION 80,000

Calgary, Alberta   August, 1931

Cover shot of *Farm and Ranch Review,* 1931. Even during the Great Depression and despite Peterson's growing pessimism, the *Farm and Ranch Review* promoted the delights of country life. In the early days its title page carried the wisdom of Socrates: "Agriculture is an employment most worthy of the application of man, the most ancient and suitable to his nature; it is the common nurse of all persons in every age and condition of life; it is the source of health, strength, plenty and riches and of a thousand sober delights and honest pleasures. It is the mistress and school of sobriety, temperance, justice, religion and, in short, of all virtues." Glenbow.

cariously, the *Review* moved from a bimonthly to monthly format, lost eleven-twelfths of its income, and then almost discontinued altogether; he released more economic pamphlets and his writing became more animated. At the same time, his conservative ethic was nearly crushed, and his confidence in the spirit of man to overcome adversity was shattered. Even his natural belief that his own experience could inform current policy was undermined.

From a distance, he viewed the collapse of the dry areas in the early twenties and remembered how the region looked like a wasteland the first time he saw it, how it resembled a paradise twenty-five years later. Pitying the suffering settlers, he praised their "marvellous demonstration of resourcefulness and staying power," and he squelched the hysteria about abandoning the south and inaugurating another ranching era. More than once, just before horrific crop disasters, he said the worst was over; more than once he told audiences that only "very circumscribed areas were totally unfit for agriculture." Often he scored relief attempts which restricted the remedies of clamoring creditors; often he upheld the sacredness of contract, albeit with the hope of enhancing rural credit facilities.[46]

Consequently, when the abandonment proceeded, he found it so distasteful, so unmanly, and so contrary to the lessons of his own experience that he dispatched his sympathy for a time and declared after seven years of devastation that "nearly all the cases of extreme distress on farms in the drought area during the past couple of years [were] due solely to mismanagement"[!][47] Deeply impressed by apparent, grave personal failings of so many settlers, he even concocted a theory of ethnic deficiency to explain why southeastern Alberta had been vacated by 1926. Those who had failed on both dry and irrigated lands were a class with too high a living standard and too grandiose a set of expectations—people from the United States, Britain and northern Europe. Plainly, he reasoned, the job of colonizing the south was one "for the hard working, frugal peasant type from eastern Europe, used to similar, or more unfavourable conditions at home."[48]

Most of these initial reactions and even the last deliberation, Peterson relinquished in time. By May 1933, the halo had left above the holy contract. "...When the individual, or the community through no fault of his own, faces a world upheaval, which renders it impossible to meet obligations," he now said, "...it is idle to talk about 'the pound of flesh.'"[49] During the Depression the dry regions were no longer "sub-humid" but "semi-arid," and they were no longer "rich beyond measure" but poor beyond belief. By early 1938, the unarable parts were no longer extremely limited, but "large areas." These tracts, he now said perfunctorily, "must be abandoned."[50]

There was, however, at least one matter on which Peterson never changed his mind. And that was that Canada, like the United States and Scandinavia, were "all more or less in the deadly grip of organized racketeers pursuing their rapacious and destructive ends, without the least regard for a perishing agriculture or the welfare of other classes."[51] For most of the past three hundred years, he wrote, a bushel of wheat had purchased four days of a skilled worker's time. In 1939 it took sixty-four bushels. *The world's highest hourrates of wages and the lowest wheat prices in centuries,* he cried from the depths of his being, *cannot exist within the same economic orbit.* Farmers had become "economic outcasts...reduced to a level of living not far removed from serfdom."[52]

As agriculture lay in ruins on the eve of the Second World War, such was the fate of the greatest occupational group in the world. Nothing could have been further from the hopes and dreams a generation before.

For Peterson and others, the preceding two decades had featured a cascade of calamity and criticism, an effusion of diviners and soothsayers, and the profoundest introspection of a century. Amid the cacophony, the editor could perhaps be forgiven for the increasing stridency of his pronouncements and the aura of gloom that had settled on his mind.

Notes

1. Arthur Meighen to Mrs. C.W. Peterson, February 7, 1944, in Mrs. Peterson's possession.
2. Peterson speeches, Lumberman's Convention, Winnipeg, 1924, Peterson papers [hereafter PP] f3, Glenbow [hereafter G].
3. Peterson speeches, Imperial Press Conference, London, November 12, 1932, PP, f6, G.
4. A.O. MacRae, *History of the Province of Alberta*, Vol. 2 (The Western Canada History Co., 1912), p. 620; PP inventory, G.; C.W. Peterson, "A Retrospect," *Farm and Ranch Review* [hereafter FRR] Jan. 20, 1921, p. 8.
5. James H. Miller, *Bibliography of Handwriting Analysis: A Graphological Index* (Troy, N.Y.: The Whitston Publishing Co., 1982), p. 5, quoting E.H. Alten. This bibliography comprises many hundreds of studies in several languages.
6. W. David Barregar, handwriting analysis of C.W. Peterson script, 1986.
7. Mrs. Else Peterson, interview, February 25, 1986, Calgary, Alberta; Eric McGreer interview, April 9, 1986, Calgary, Alberta.
8. Eric McGreer interview.
9. Peterson, "Editorial Problems," *FRR*, December 10, 1917, p. 5.
10. Peterson, "Public Opinion," *FRR*, February 1932, p. 6; Peterson, *Wake Up, Canada! Reflections on Vital National Issues* (Toronto: Macmillan, 1919), p. 1.
11. Ibid., pp. 171–76.
12. Ibid., pp. 17–20.
13. Ibid., p. 154.
14. Ibid., p. 262.
15. Peterson, "The Live Stock Outlook," *FRR*, December 20, 1915, p. 728.
16. David C. Jones, *Empire of Dust—Settling and Abandoning the Prairie Dry Belt* (Edmonton: University of Alberta Press, 1987), p. 212.
17. Peterson, "The Irrigation Problem," *FRR*, May 1937, p. 20.
18. Peterson, "Political Tolerance," *FRR*, June 10, 1925, p. 5.
19. Peterson, "A Controlled Press," *FRR*, February 21, 1921, p. 7.
20. Peterson, "The Age of Bunk," *FRR*, October 20, 1922, p. 5.
21. Peterson, "Political Nobodies," *FRR*, February 20, 1920, p. 5.
22. Peterson, "The U.F.A. Convention," *FRR*, February 5, 1923, p. 5.
23. Peterson, "The Age of Bunk," p. 5.
24. Peterson, "Political Nobodies," p. 5.
25. Peterson, "Rainbow Chasing," *FRR*, March 5, 1921, p. 8.

26. Peterson, "Western Grain Marketing and the Great Betrayal," *FRR*, August 6, 1923, p. 3.

27. Editor, "Prayer and Mr. Peterson," *The U.F.A.*, September 1, 1923, p. 11.

28. H.W. Wood, "Mr. Peterson," *The U.F.A.*, October 15, 1923, p. 12.

29. Peterson, "Mr. Wood and His Personal Organ," *FRR*, October 5, 1923, p. 5.

30. Peterson, "The New Year," *FRR*, December 20, 1923, p. 5.

31. Peterson, "Mr. H.W. Wood Re-Elected U.F.A. President," *FRR*, January 25, 1924, p. 5.

32. C.W. Peterson, *The Fruits of the Earth: A Story of the Canadian Prairies* (Ottawa: Ru-Mi-Lou Books, 1928), pp. 277, 280–81.

33. Peterson, "Evolution or Revolution," *FRR*, November 1933, p. 5; Peterson, *Wake Up, Canada!* pp. 12–13.

34. Peterson, drafts of articles, "Economic Value of Genious," 1938c., PP, f2, G.

35. Peterson, "The U.F.A. Platform," *FRR*, August 1932, p. 6.

36. Peterson, "The Socialist Paradise," *FRR*, November 1938, pp. 5–6.

37. Peterson, "Another Raid on Agriculture," *FRR*, September 10, 1927, p. 5. Peterson appeared less certain of this point in *Wake Up, Canada!* See p. 323, and supra, p. 172.

38. Peterson, "Where the Shoe Pinches," *FRR*, January 25, 1926, p. 5.

39. Peterson, "The Crow's Nest Agreement, The Railway Situation and Railway Labour," *FRR*, May 5, 1922, p. 5.

40. Peterson, "Farmer-Labour Government and Labour Legislation," *FRR*, April 10, 1924, p. 6. Peterson appeared somewhat more tolerant of miners in *Wake Up, Canada!* See p. 168 and supra, p. 81.

41. Peterson, "Who Controls Freight Rates?" *FRR*, January 10, 1925, p. 5.

42. C.W. Peterson, *Social Credit: A Critical Analysis* (Calgary: Published by the author, 1937), p. 4, italics in the original.

43. Reg Carlile to Mrs. Else Peterson, February 8, 1944, in Mrs. Peterson's possession.

44. Peterson, "More Light and Less Heat," *FRR*, July 1937, p. 5.

45. Ibid.

46. Peterson, "The Dry Land Pioneer," *FRR*, August 20, 1921, p. 7; "A Statesman Has Arisen," *FRR*, February 6, 1922, p. 5; "The Testing Time," *FRR*, March 6, 1922, p. 5; "The State of Agriculture in the Sub-Humid Areas," *FRR*, March 6, 1922, p. 6; "The Problem of the Sub-Humid Districts," *FRR*, June 20, 1923, p. 5.

47. Peterson, "Living and Boarding at Home," *FRR*, September 20, 1923, p. 6.

48. Peterson, "Canada and the Closed Door," *FRR*, April 26, 1926, p. 5;
    Peterson speeches, Lethbridge, Alberta, [1921], PP, f3, G; Lethbridge,
    Alberta, May 1926, PP, f6, G; Calgary, Alberta, June 1926, PP, f6, G.
49. Peterson, "Debts and Interest," *FRR*, May 1933, p. 5.
50. Peterson, "The Drouth Areas," *FRR*, February 1938, pp. 5–6.
51. Peterson speeches, Olds, Alberta, June 1940, PP, F3, G.
52. Peterson, "The Economics of Guaranteed Wheat Prices," *FRR*, May
    1939, pp. 5–6.

WAKE UP, CANADA!

To the Editors
of Canadian Newspapers
and Periodicals

PREFACE

I regretfully realize that this is a scolding, preaching, fault-finding sort of book, only mildly constructive. And Canada is not used to having her institutions libelled in book form. In Great Britain, on the other hand, every week or so, some unlicensed crank writes a volume on how to run the Empire, which, of course, no one ever takes seriously. The patronage and encouragement of this literary Hyde Park speaks volumes for the patriotism of British publishers! However, the precedent is now set in Canada, for better or for worse.

It will be obvious to those who are sufficiently interested to read the following pages that it is not the mission of this volume to submit cut and dried remedies for the various ills and handicaps, social, political, and economic, under which Canada labours. Many of them are common to all countries. My object is rather to bring some of our problems to the attention of thinking people, to contribute in a mild measure to intelligent discussion and to spur into action those whose responsibility it is to solve them. But, above everything, it is my earnest ambition to rouse Canadian men and women from their present apathetic attitude in regard to the politics and administration of the country and to kindle an intelligent interest in the great questions of the day.

I love this Canada of ours—this clean, strenuous, blessed, young country, seemingly so enormously distant from the slimy, unwholesome social mess of Europe. But one cannot shut one's eyes to the evidence of unrest apparent even here. It is the main purpose of this book to contribute, to a modest extent, towards the awakening of Canada to a sense of her responsibilities and opportunities. We must look past errors bravely in the face and energetically turn our attention to setting the house in order. Herein will lie Canada's salvation and her ability to fulfil her God-given destiny of becoming the haven of refuge for oppressed people, and for those adventurous spirits who chafe at the restraints of older civilizations.

C.W.P.
Western Stock Ranches
Calgary, Alberta
April, 1919

ONE

Democracy on Trial

THE AMAZING CATACLYSM into which a peaceful world was precipitated in 1914 ultimately gained such proportions that the normal life of the individual the world over was affected to a greater or lesser extent. Carefully treasured economic theories have been blasted into utter oblivion. Nations are drifting like rudderless ships on the high seas. Patching here and mending there, some hope to sail into safe havens. Others lie bleeding and mangled while irrepressible mobs put to the torch the outward and visible evidences of centuries of slow and laborious progress and civilization.

If one does not misread all the signs and tokens, the end of this bloody war is ushering in a new era all over the civilized world. We shall be taught to renounce many things that the present generation has most admired in men; wealth, power, position and fame, and to estimate men and things at their true worth. The drone will be an outcast. He probably will not have the wealth to enable him to lead the drone's existence. The State will require it. The man who does things will be the leader—not the man whose only claim to distinction is that he made a happy choice of parents.

The conviction is forcing itself on thoughtful observers that the past world struggle and its aftermath is less a trial of strength between the autocratic and democratic ideas of Government, than a fire trial of democracy itself. The world has now decided that autocracies must go, not necessarily because they are inefficient, but because they are irresponsible.

◆

What about the world's democracies? Have they fulfilled the reasonable expectations of the early pioneers of liberty, fraternity and equality? Have they abolished sweated and child labour and all the other abominations of our industrial system? If these conditions have from time to time been ameliorated, has it been by the voluntary action of the State or by the power of organized labour forcing its demands on reluctant democracy? Has democracy abolished the pest-ridden tenements of our great cities? Can, in fact, democracy show that the status of the common people has been higher and better under its beneficent rule than it was in the autocratic countries we have just defeated? Let us look the facts straight in the face.

Let us also remember that democracy has, in some countries, abolished an hereditary aristocracy and has substituted therefor a plutocracy, with swollen fortunes made out of the sweat of the brow of its citizens. The aristocrat was generally actuated by the *noblesse oblige* principle and frequently rendered patriotic public services. The plutocrat, on the other hand, has for his own selfish purposes, debauched our public life and even spread the net of graft among the people's representatives. Are we the better for the change? Democracy—government for the people, by the people—has been on the job for over a century and, frankly, has it proven so vastly superior as a political scheme that the transformation from autocracy to our alleged advanced system is merely a matter of form? Do we not detect in the liberated countries an ever-swelling rejection of the sort of democracy that has in the past satisfied our consciences? We apparently cannot comprehend that any nation just emerging from the darkness of autocracy should contain any considerable element of people who would hesitate to adopt holus-bolus our own scheme of Government. Yet, it is so. And not alone is it so, but these new notions are not confined to the conquered. They are being rapidly assimilated among the conquerors. Read and digest the following from a speech by a Canadian at Toronto:

We advocate the dictatorship of the people or proletariat. Under this creed society must be turned upside down, the will of the workers being imposed on the "bourgeoise," or ruling class. The State, as it exists today, must be destroyed, and with it must go overboard law and all the political institutions of the country, for we maintain that these exist only to oppress the poor and protect the ruling class. In place of the State the Bolshevist places the revolution organization of the workers. The first duty of that body is to dispossess the capitalists, take control of all key industries, land, mines, railways, means of postal and telegraph communication and the newspapers, and run them for the benefit of the workers and the extension of the Bolshevist system. The land is to be parcelled out and given to the peasants free of tenure. The factories are taken over without compensation to owners or shareholders, to be run by shop committees. All profits from whatever source are to be administered by a Central Revolutionary Committee until such time as they are handed over to the workers. The Bolshevists lay down a dogma that the workers at all costs are supreme, and to attain this end all means are justifiable. . . .

And thus the Bolshevist is endeavouring to create a limbo large and broad, since called "The Paradise of Fools."

The conflict of arms in the cradle of modern civilization has mercifully ceased. But where heroes have gallantly spilled their life blood in defence of all that makes life sweet and desirable, drivelling anarchy is rearing its leering, vacant face. Frightened Europe stands aghast.

Eighty per cent of the people have little or nothing to lose in any violent social upheaval. The remaining twenty per cent own it all. Those in the former category may be tempted to try any creed, any experiment, and, moblike, be carried away by it.

Let us not, however, for a moment imagine that Bolshevism is something copied from a comic opera—that there is no rational, dominating idea behind the seemingly crazy performances of the adherents of this new and extraordinary creed. If there were not, it would simply subside by its own efforts and might properly be treated as an unusually widespread outbreak of lunacy. What is it? An American, recently returned from Petrograd where he had occupied an official position in behalf of his own country, expressed to the writer his utter lack of sympathy with the much persecuted bourgeoisie of Russia. It was bad and reactionary to the core. He was most pessimistic about the whole political prospect in that country. He was apparently convinced that the elements of true democracy were not in the bourgeoisie of Russia and could not be instilled into that class. Their point of view was utterly and hopelessly at variance with that of the humbler classes.

This statement tells its own story. The Maximalist has no intention of spending a century or two in educating the classes. His creed is death and destruction and the rearing of a new structure of State on the ruins of the old order of society. It is inhuman and cruel, but there is method and purpose in the seeming madness. It is devoid of all the finer instincts and lofty aspirations of our modern civilization; it is ruthless and it is relentless; it is something we never pictured even in our most horrid night-mares. It is a world scarlet with blood and fire!

◆

On this side of the Atlantic we may escape the rocks and reefs of the older civilizations of Europe. In Canada and the United States, while individual fortunes may in many cases be enormous, the rank and file are not devoid of property. Two-thirds of the farmers in the United States own their holdings. In Canada the proportion is much greater. In the smaller towns and cities the labourer frequently owns his home. The future holds greater promise over here. The industrious bricklayer of to-day is often the successful contractor of to-morrow. Such conditions are unfavourable to violent reconstruction. They are not necessarily unfavourable to far-reaching social reform.

If we in Canada escape the doom of the countries of Central Europe, let us, in all humility, confess our past sins of omission and commission, and determine to use our talents in a manner more worthy of the destiny of this great virgin country that the Almighty has handed over to us in trust for future generations.

If Bolshevism devoured us, it would be perhaps only retributive justice for a century of soft living, of selfish ambitions, of grinding poverty here and ostentatious luxury there; the prostitution and caricaturing of the stage, "jazz band" music, our lascivious, erotic literature, and monstrous, degenerate modern schools of art, of forgetting to be "our brother's keeper"—of general failure to use our new-found political liberty in the interests of humanity, education and arts, and of misusing it for the promotion of private greed and in riotous living.

Democracy has been pulled up with a sharp turn. Democratic Europe has heedlessly proceeded on its way, lulled and soothed into foolish security by the comfortable conviction that all was well. Were they not in Great Britain, for instance, good citizens of a free country? But democracies built on a social system that has rendered it possible for a few to accumulate fabulous fortunes while multitudes have lived in misery, filth and starvation—a social system that has given into the hands of the few, however deserving, hard working and superior they may be, the ownership or stewardship of all the things that represent power over the fate of the majority—a social system which, by virtually denying the average man a stake in the community, has gradually produced a proletariat devoid of all sense of responsibility for the maintenance of the existing order—such a democracy, I say, is perhaps in greater danger of utter annihilation than the vilest of autocracies. It rests not on a solid foundation, but on a veritable volcano.

Individual benevolence by the possessors of swollen fortunes—restitution to society—will not meet the case. The breadwinner is clamouring for steady employment and for protection against the economic consequences of illness, accident and death. He asks for bread and he is given books—libraries of them!

The gradual development, among the nations of the world, of all the vices and evils to which ancient Rome ultimately fell a victim, is not a pleasant retrospect. In the larger cities of Canada and the

United States, where the social unrest is most noticeable, the past twenty years have been a period of "easy" money, and reckless, offensive spending. Business men have developed wolfish instincts. Many of our statesmen—the noblest calling of all—have degenerated into "practical" politicians. The gratification of social ambition has been, amongst our women of the "classes," one of the main objects in life, with the aping of the habits of the very wealthy and so on down the list. The showy "front" has been a subject of emulation. The expenditure on personal adornment must surely have made our grandmothers turn in their graves. And our smart establishments! The modest carriage and pair has been replaced by fleets of expensive motor cars. Haughty, pale-faced children, who would be vastly benefited by fresh air and healthful exercise, are carried to school in luxurious limousines with uniformed chauffeurs, passing the offspring of the mechanic, trudging through the snow, and casting envious eyes on these darlings of fortune.

Let us offer up devout gratitude that grim war at last stepped in and laid its heavy hand upon our heedless society, spurred us to action, and brought out all that was best and noblest within us. The social butterfly went to work. The spendthrift stopped spending. Weary years of ceaseless worry and heavy responsibility opened our eyes to the worth-while things in life. We see and read more understandingly now that the spirit of charity and toleration has descended upon us. We realize that there is enough and plenty in this good old world of ours, so that we may all have the necessaries of life and some of its comforts and luxuries. And many of us even dimly perceive that we all came naked into this existence, whether in cottage or mansion, and will leave it in the same condition; that no class among us is God's chosen—a peculiar people; but that we are all just very ordinary, average, miserable sinners, whose duty and privilege it is to wander through life, lending a hand to help the weaker brother over rough places, faithfully performing our allotted tasks and, finally, making our exit, dwelling in our last moments with satisfaction only upon the sum of our services to others. Upon our ability to see these things clearly may depend our future status as a nation.

———◆———

At this period, the whole scheme of democratic government seems
to drift between Scylla and Charybdis. During the past decades, nations have apparently progressed farther in the field of political
freedom than in education and fitness for the great responsibilities
incidental to citizenship in the ideal democracy. It has been well
said that the step from pure democracy to tyrannous autocracy is
surprisingly easily made. The proletariat calls out loudly for the in-
auguration of the Social State. It is mistakenly being regarded as
synonymous with the widest political emancipation, with which it
has absolutely nothing to do. They have it in Russia. How do you
like it? Wherein lies the difference between Kaiser Wilhelm and
Trotsky? Bismarck has often been characterized as the most advanced and practical socialist of his time. And he was. Germany
had unemployment insurance and all the rest of it. It was almost a
socialized state—and yet a nation of abject, cringing slaves.

This idealization of the socialized state has become a menace to
civilization. We do not seem to comprehend, except in the haziest
manner, that consistent socialization is absolutely incompatible
with individual liberty of action, the boon most highly prized by the
true democrat. We see it clearly demonstrated all around us. The
multiplication of Government functions, promoted largely by our
tendency towards the socialized State, is rapidly driving our modern democracies into tyranny. We are denied, right and left, the
basic privilege of self-determination.

This complete surrender of self-determination and individual
liberty, which is involved in the socialized State; this submission is
being drynursed and shepherded from birth to death by a paternal
governmental authority; this smug wholesale insuring against all
the calamities and vicissitudes of life; this tender shielding and
guarding of the individual from all the temptations that beset red-
blooded men and women—what sort of a race of human beings will
it breed? Shall we not lose all our powers of initiative and foresight,
our capacity for fighting, bravely and manfully, against the odds
and evils of life? Shall we not become a nation of hypocrites,

secretly breaking irksome restrictions? Shall we not finally become imbued with a contempt for all laws as a result of failure to rigidly enforce some of them? In a measure we are deliberately attempting to circumvent the operation of the eternal law of the survival of the fittest. We are trying by Act of Parliament to prevent the weakling from utterly destroying himself, and every time he discovers a new way of attempting it, which he inevitably will, we pass a new Act of Parliament! Is there no longer within us any response to the spiritual appeal? Have we not reached the point in democracy when the principal business of the State appears to be to busy itself with our petty vices? The fate of great political parties ought not to hang on such issues. And now we are promised a crusade against cigarettes, two per cent beer and cent-a-point bridge! Is this the higher civilization?

TWO

Canadian Nationality

CANADA IS A COUNTRY of dual language and dual nationality. Under the terms of Confederation, certain rights were guaranteed the French Canadians in respect of the official use of the French language. That fact seems to worry a great many people. A literature has grown up around this question, and some otherwise sane people seem to see in this equitable, fair and highly satisfactory arrangement, a menace to Canada and a brake on progress. It never seems to occur to these people that the situation is very far from unique. Belgium has two languages, Switzerland has three. Every country in Europe has dialects almost as strange as a foreign tongue. Certainly, if we have a language problem it can only be due to narrow prejudice, bad management, and unscrupulous political agitation.

It seems almost superfluous to state the fact that a strong, virile nation can be successfully created out of peoples speaking different tongues. In many ways a dual language is very advantageous or could be made so. If every child in Canada spoke English and French with equal fluency, the country would unquestionably be the gainer. Art, literature and general culture, would be immeasurably promoted to the vast benefit of us all. Amalgamation of tribes and races into nations is a process that has been going merrily on as far back as recorded history is available. On the surface, there seems to be nothing particular to worry about in our case. The thing is to study each other's point of view, to be mutually sympathetic and, above all, to practise courtesy and toleration.

◆

Jean Baptiste is not a fighting man. He is essentially domestic, and the spirit of adventure does not exist in the present generation of French-Canadians. Leave his aged mother, or his wife and children, and go across the ocean to offer up his life for a principle, and a dollar and ten cents a day? Did one ever hear of such madness? When conscription was delicately hinted at, the French press went into hysterics. Rapine and rebellion, battle, murder and sudden death would be the inevitable answer in Quebec. The streets of the cities would flow with the blood of the oppressors. When the order ultimately went into effect, Jean, like the simple, decent, law-abiding citizen that he is, came into the fold like a lamb and cheerfully went to the Front. That is, any stray Jean who had been utterly unable to satisfy a very, very complaisant board that he really ought to be exempted, which he, by the way, seldom failed to do.

French Quebec's contribution towards winning the war was, therefore, not conspicuous. The French-Canadian units that went across, however, covered themselves with glory, as the entire French-Canadian population would doubtless have done, had it been there. The fact of the matter is that the habitant, the real French-Canadian, lives in a sixteenth century atmosphere. Quebec is his country, and Monsieur le Curé is a deputy god. Great Britain and France actually mean no more to him than Nova Scotia or Saskatchewan—and that is nothing at all. The Province of Quebec should really educate this man and make a real citizen of him. There is no better raw material anywhere.

In the meanwhile, let there be no illusions in this matter. The guttersnipes and sweepings of the slums of Montreal, even the ranting college professors, hysterical politicians and radical newspaper editors of the French element, do not represent French Canada. We are apt to think they do, and they think so themselves, but they really do not. Even Ottawa, which ought to know better, trembled before

these men. No national question whatever could be decided without deep consideration as to how Quebec would take it. The small
group of French-speaking Ministers was always able to block any
plan or policy, no matter how meritorious, by a mere intimation
that Quebec would not like it. The cabinet soon became frightened
at its own shadow. It was almost completely dominated by this element. In course of time, the French Ministers and members naturally began to take themselves seriously. The balance of power
depended on Quebec. No government could lightly ignore this situation.

But the last election broke the spell. Canada has now found out
that she can get on comfortably, practically without French representation in the cabinet. Rebellion did not break out, nor famine
visit the land. Now apparently it does not matter a row of pins how
Quebec takes anything, which is precisely the mental attitude that is
best for Canada, especially for Quebec. No single province will ever
dominate Canada again. It is unhealthy.

I have great hopes for the future of that splendid race. They are
god-fearing, hard-working and law-abiding people, reasonably
prosperous, very contented, and faithful to the command of their
church to people the earth. Why is it that the Roman Catholic
church, for which I personally entertain the deepest admiration, respect and regard, never can quite forget the old days of temporal
jurisdiction? Why must it always either occupy the throne or be the
power behind the throne? Look at Quebec, look at Ireland. It is a
pity that this venerable, hoary institution that has emerged triumphantly from the ashes of every wild holocaust the world has
ever witnessed, cannot learn to confine its activities to the spiritual
and moral elevation of its adherents, and leave political intrigue
and strife to less worthy agencies. Perhaps it is because this great organization cultivates the martyr spirit. The Roman Catholic church
is said to thrive on persecution.

◆

The United States is a nation with a flag. It is a compact, definite,
national unit with a history and traditions behind it and with an in-

tense patriotism and pride of country pervading all classes. There is no divided or dual allegiance. An American is an American.

Canada, on the other hand, is the dutiful and admiring daughter of the greatest Mother of Nations. The flag is Mother's. Ask an English-born citizen, who has perhaps spent many years in Canada, whether he is a Canadian, and he will smile. He is, of course, an Englishman or a Britisher. Ask a New Zealand born colonist in Canada as to his nationality and he will reply that he is a New Zealander. A foreign-born, naturalized citizen may tell you that he is a Canadian. But without further formalities he is not a Britisher. Only a small fraction of native Canadians ever visit the shores of Great Britain. It seems that we are endeavouring to cultivate in Canada a sense of dual-nationality. Our status is beclouded and intangible. Can we readily assimilate foreign populations on such a basis?

It seems clear that a more distinct sense of Canadian nationality must be developed amongst us, sooner or later, or we shall partly fail in our mission to provide homes for multitudes from overseas and elsewhere. We cannot be satisfied with the position of a "polyglot boarding-house." We must either keep strangers out, or we must assimilate them. There must be no half measures.

THREE

Political Parties and Classes

THE PRESENT POLITICAL situation in Canada is absolutely chaotic. Old affiliations have been ruthlessly sundered, new problems of public administration are arising almost daily and the time, of course, is inopportune for the construction of permanent political platforms, around which the voters might rally, according to their convictions. The whole political horizon is, to say the least, obscure. Class organization is proceeding with rapidity, and political views are slowly crystallizing. For the first time in the history of Canada, there is a distinct tendency towards the multiplication of political parties on a basis of organized effort. Class consciousness is unmistakably developing in Canada and will, of necessity, exercise a tremendous influence upon the political situation.

◆

The most far-reaching class organization is undoubtedly the "Grain Growers" or "Farmers' Union" movement. This had a modest beginning in 1899 in the then North-West Territories. Since then it has spread all through the Prairie Provinces and also to Ontario. The strength of this movement lies in the very fact that it has not been developed for political, but primarily for business purposes. The former is purely incidental. This means that the membership is tied up to the organization by motives of commercial self-interest, and as the organization has so far been an outstanding success from a business point of view, it rests on a vastly more solid foundation than that of a mere political body. This organization is, therefore, one distinctly to be reckoned with in the future. And it has views— most uncomfortable views for any political party that looks for support among the industrial classes of Canada, particularly those of Ontario and Quebec. Its pronouncements on public questions are frequently intolerant, uncompromising and extreme. One sometimes detects traces of internationalism and socialism in its debates and utterances. But the scatterbrains are gradually being eliminated and wiser counsels will ultimately prevail.

The farmers of Canada, representing as they do, the largest class of property owners in the Dominion, will doubtless recognize, sooner or later, that their true interests lie in promoting safe and sane conditions, and that they are diametrically opposed to experimental legislation and all the political and social nostrums that so-called advanced thinkers are now endeavouring to incorporate in their platform and propaganda. The trouble in the past has been that the movement has been largely in the hands of idealists and enthusiasts—honest and well-meaning men, but lacking balance and political perspicuity. A change already in progress may be looked for in the radical views that now seem to prevail among the leaders.

Another and most important political factor is, of course, that of organized labour. While this class only numbers about 160,000 members in Canada, or, approximately, 20 per cent of all Canadian workers, skilled and unskilled, the movement is exceedingly well organized and widely distributed throughout Canada. The platform of organized labour is frankly international and socialistic, although not officially so, as far as the latter is concerned. Organized labour has always been a factor of weight in Canadian politics, but no separate political party has ever been formed to represent this class. What the future has in store in this respect is doubtful. It is certain that organized labour has in the past exercised a far more powerful influence on legislation, acting through accredited leaders, than could have been the case if direct representation in Parliament had been sought. It is possible that the same policy may be followed in the future, but there are indications of a desire to form a labour party. There have, of course, been local attempts made to run labour candidates in Dominion and Provincial elections and in many cases they have been successful, but the organization, as a whole, has lent no active official support in such cases.

It is curious that Canada has almost entirely escaped class representation in its popular legislative bodies. Various countries in Europe have for years had agrarian parties to safeguard the interests of agriculture and the land-owning classes.

A comparatively new element has been projected into politics during recent years, namely, the woman voter. Party managers are very much at sea as to the outcome of it all. It is a great experiment.

The country has a right to expect from its women an uncompromising attitude with regard to purity of public life, and sympathetic consideration and support of all rational policies that will promote the greatest good of the greatest number of our citizens. The women of Canada should acquaint themselves with public questions, and should regard the franchise as a sacred trust, exercising it with a sense of great responsibility.

◆

The notorious preponderance of lawyers in public life in Canada is very curious. The superstition seems to prevail that this class is, in some way, specially qualified for public life. This is open to the strongest possible doubt. Apart from the general educational qualifications, and it must be admitted that the average lawyer is a well educated man, lawyers as a class are not endowed with more than average business qualifications—in fact, many claim that the average lawyer is not a good business man.

The following table shows the occupations of the men in the Dominion and Provincial legislative bodies.

A glance at this table shows a peculiar state of affairs. The lawyers, numbering less than 5,000 in the whole of Canada, and being only a fraction of the population, monopolize 25 per cent of the total representation. Labour is practically unrepresented, while the

OCCUPATIONS OF PARLIAMENTARY REPRESENTATIVES IN CANADA

	Lawyers	Other Professions	Merchants and Industries	Labour	Farmers	Total Representation
Senate of Canada	24	18	40	1	11	94
House of Commons	79	47	72	1	32	231
Nova Scotia	16	13	27	—	1	57
Prince Edward Island	4	3	17	—	6	30
New Brunswick	11	8	22	—	6	48
Quebec	37	16	41	—	9	103
Ontario	22	21	43	—	21	107
Manitoba	7	12	17	1	10	50
Saskatchewan	5	4	12	1	38	60
Alberta	9	11	16	—	22	58
British Columbia	8	10	22	1	5	46
	222	163	329	5	161	884

farmer class, almost half the entire adult population, only have about 18 per cent of the representation. There are four vacancies.

◆

In the political game of the "ins and outs" that has, until recently, been played in Canada, the "machinery" has been developed to a very fine point. Members have been given cabinet rank and placed in charge of important portfolios frankly because they knew how to play this game. The fact that Governments have remained in power for from 12 to 18 years, in spite of records that should have consigned them to oblivion, is ample evidence of the fact that means have been placed in the hands of the Government of the day to defy public opinion and to prevent a true expression of such opinion at the polls.

In the raising of party funds for the purpose of defraying election expenses, one comes face to face with graft in its most pernicious form. In the old days, votes sold to the highest bidder, and this barefaced corruption of the electorate excited only a mild form of protest. The crime was largely in being found out.

Nowadays, the evil lies rather in the method of raising election funds than in the expenditure thereof. When a general election is impending, the party managers set to work to obtain the sinews of war. The hat is passed. It comes to the "Universal Steel Co." if there is such a concern. The Board of Directors makes a large subscription, and covers the payment up in its books. Why? Is this corporation making a contribution as a patriotic Canadian concern, purely in the interest of good government? Or is it in anticipation of favours to come? It is perhaps enjoying heavy protection under our fiscal system and desires to be left undisturbed. Or perhaps it has a "case" and is looking for an increase. In order to guard against all possible eventualities, however, when the "hat" from the opposition side comes round the next day, the Directors determine on a "safety first" policy, and make an equally large contribution. Thus both sides are squared. This is how it works.

It is unnecessary to enlarge on the cruder and criminal arrangements under which certain sums are added to Government contracts to cover "extras" and are afterwards transferred to the party "slush" fund by the grateful beneficiaries. During quite recent years, deals of this sort, carried out in the rawest possible manner, have seen the light of day, following criminal proceedings.

———————◆———————

Everyone regrets the power and activities of the party "machine." "Machine" government naturally follows "machine" won elections. Let us examine the "machine" and see how it works. It organizes meetings, personally canvasses the voters and distributes, in printed form, special pleadings in favour of the party. This is quite legitimate. Then comes the election day. Now, supposing the machine remained inactive on that day of days? As a first result, we should probably get a fair expression of a limited popular opinion at the polls. But half of the voters would not vote!

This is where the "machine" puts in its most effective work, in bringing the vote out to the poll. This saves labour—to the voter. Each "machine," of course, brings out the people only that will vote for the party it represents, and will often go to some lengths in keeping opponents at home. Let us be quite frank about it, however unpalatable the truth may be. The result of any election, unless some great public question is involved, depends almost entirely upon the degree of field organization and financial means available in bringing the favourable vote out on election day. Boiled down to its logical conclusions, it means that the average voter is too lazy or too indifferent to go to the poll unless a comfortable conveyance calls for him, takes him there and then brings him home again.

Is the franchise a privilege, or a duty? This question goes to the root of the whole matter. If a privilege, those who are too indifferent to avail themselves of it might properly be disenfranchised. This would lead to an intelligent expression of public opinion. If a duty, everyone failing to perform that duty, unless prevented from voting by some serious obstacle, should be dealt with as an offender. This means compulsory voting. The moment we had compulsory voting, the "machine" would be largely confined to its legitimate object, which is to educate public opinion to the views of the party it represents. The final expression of public opinion would thus be left absolutely unhampered, and would really represent public opinion and not machine-made opinion. If we had compulsory voting and proportional representation, we could perhaps dispense with all the other innovations, and feel reasonably certain that the party in power, be it good, bad or indifferent truly represented the consensus of public opinion. And that is the utmost demand that a democracy can make.

Sickness or absolutely unavoidable business elsewhere should be the only excuses accepted for failure to vote. A Justice of the Peace could hold court after election day in each polling division and quickly determine the merits of each excuse. Disenfranchisement for a certain period, and a small fine, should be meted out to delinquents. This system would quickly break the back of "machine" politics.

We have certain very plain duties as citizens of a democracy. If we do not want to discharge these duties and contribute our quota towards good and honest government, we are unfit for the privileges of a citizen of a democracy. We might as well be in Germany, or under some other autocracy, where the plain citizen, as far as responsibility for good government is concerned, ranks with the Canadian minor or lunatic. Another century of educating may be needed before we shall properly value the franchise and realize our duty as citizens.

———————◆———————

It is instructive to watch the total vote cast for each party in an election, and compare this with the number of representatives, elected, of each party. Generally these figures bear absolutely no proper proportion to each other. In other words, majority rule under the present system very largely eliminates minority representation. Proportional representation is designed to arrive at a fairer expression of the will of the voter at the polls. It is now quite possible for a political party to have a large majority in Parliament without actually having polled a majority of the votes throughout the country.

———————◆———————

The reconstruction period upon which we have now entered, will make large demands upon cooperation between Dominion and Provincial authorities. The labour and employment policy is founded on team work; the soldiers' settlement and re-establishment work likewise. Great colonization policies can only be worked out under joint control. There is every indication that a new administrative era is dawning, involving the closest co-operation between Provincial and Federal authorities, and no such silly obstacle as political "machinery" should be permitted to stand in the way of the fullest realization of the great possibilities of such a movement.

———————◆———————

And a word as to the private member, federal and provincial. The whole system of party government, involving party discipline, to some extent enforced by party contributions towards election expenses, has had the effect of reducing our representatives to mere voting machines. The few that have the temerity to strike an independent attitude on some great question run the risk of utter political annihilation. The House doesn't like insurrection. Of course, his opportunity comes in the party caucus where he can criticize to his heart's content, behind closed doors in secret session. But in broad daylight the party must vote as a unit, whether on one side of the house of the other. All this, of course, is not conducive to efficiency, but it is the system. In effect, the private member might as well return home immediately after the caucus and leave the detail to the leaders. He has become an absolute automaton. The good old days when governments could be defeated on the Floor of Parliament have long ago departed. Our present system does not admit of any such eventuality. The "machine" works too smoothly.

The present system is absolutely demoralizing. It leaves no scope for individual originality or ingenuity. The private member attends the sessions of Parliament perfunctorily. He is not there to listen to argument and weigh measures in the balance, intelligently and impartially, and act on his convictions as our constitution contemplated. His mission is merely to obey the call of the party whip and to vote as he is told and in general, to play the party game loyally. It is difficult to see how this evil can be entirely overcome under our system of party government. To elect men imbued with a sense of patriotic duty rather than a desire to slavishly submit to party dictation, if such men can be found and could be nominated, would be a further step towards improvement.

Our blind adherence to political parties has beyond all doubt been largely responsible for most of the past expensive administrative blunders in Canada. It is, however, refreshing to note a healthy reaction in this respect as a direct result of the influence on the public mind of the Great War. The spectacle of the vast majority of staunch Canadian liberals cheerfully joining hands with the opposite party for the purpose of supporting a coalition administration, under conservative leadership, to pilot the ship of State through a great world crisis, is perhaps the most promising and inspiring in the political history of Canada. It clearly demonstrated that, at the core, the electorate is sound.

FOUR

Business Government

THERE WAS NEVER A period in the history of the world more fruitful of new notions in government than the present. There is scarcely a public meeting held anywhere nowadays that does not give birth to a new idea. The superstition seems to have taken hold of people that the only reconstruction that society needs is what can be provided by Act of Parliament. Church Assemblies, socialist meetings, Canadian Club luncheons, etc., each makes its contribution to the appalling unrest that is now manifest. While there are certain things Parliament can advantageously do to provide necessary machinery and organization to promote reform, the main burden must necessarily fall on the shoulders of the individual citizen, who must wake up to a realization of his duties and responsibilities to his fellowman and to the conscientious use of the ballot.

What is required in Canada today is not a set of new-fangled political, social or economic systems, but rather a complete overhauling and critical examination of the present structure, a plentiful use of the searchlight and a plentiful application of common sense, tempered with common humanity. Cold-blooded business and warm-blooded sympathy must go hand in hand and prune and plant on the way. We must elect and support statesmen of high personal integrity and purpose, but, above all, with vision and imagination. The old school of politician is as dead as Caesar's wife. May we never see his shadow again. The call has gone out for Business Government.

Canada is the most plentifully governed country in the wide world. It is a veritable Mecca of Statesmen. Even Lichtenstein and Monaco fade into utter insignificance beside Canada's dizzy record in responsible government. I hasten to explain that the burden of responsibility is deftly distributed over so many broad shoulders that, in Canada, the role of Atlas is an obsolete occupation! As a school in statesmanship, Canada can be highly recommended. With our ever-expanding, and ever-changing Governments, there is room for all, sooner or later.

Now, pay attention! We have a noble army of twenty-one members of the Dominion Cabinet and two or three Parliamentary Under-Secretaries thrown in for good measure. The Province of Ontario has nine cabinet ministers. Quebec tops the list with ten. Nova Scotia, Alberta and British Columbia have eight each, New Brunswick and Saskatchewan nine, Manitoba a modest seven. To cap the climax, that tiny little Province to the far east, Prince Edward Island, comes to the front with a solid nine ministers. This makes a total of ninety-eight full-fledged cabinet ministers in Canada. Needless to add, forty-five of them are ornaments of the legal profession. Quebec sports eight lawyers out of ten ministers. The Federal Government twelve out of twenty-one. The lawyers have it!

All this, I am aware, reads very much like a fairy-tale. Ninety-eight ministers to govern eight million people! In England a cabinet about the same size as our Dominion Privy Council takes care of a population of thirty-six millions and of an Empire containing hundreds of millions of people of all colours and creeds. In the United States a cabinet about half the size of our Federal Government looks after a population of over a hundred millions. I wonder if any other part of the civilized world can show a state of affairs to equal Canada's wanton extravagance and inefficiency in Government? It is a reproach to our business sense.

But the worst feature of it all is that everyone of these Cabinets and Parliaments, and "near" Cabinets and Parliaments, must put on the usual "swank." Great piles of magnificent buildings grace the various provincial capitals. Millions upon millions have been added to the provincial public debt in order that one province might outshine another and provide flashy surroundings for our army of ministers and our 884 legislators. The Province of Manitoba is now completing its Parliament buildings at a cost of over seven million dollars, while the farmers, in many districts of that province, wade through mud to get their produce to market! And each province has its own petty Court—imitation royalty—also set in a suitable and expensive frame. The Lieutenant-Governor, of course, has, normally, nothing to do but sign his name, a function which the Chief Justice of each Province could most efficiently and economically perform, thus saving the country much absolutely useless expense.

◆

I entertain the hope that some day a capable writer will give to the world the administrative history of the North-West Territories of the old days, then comprising the Districts of Assiniboia, Saskatchewan and Alberta. That administration might well serve as a model of economical and efficient government to be studied by all who aspire to cabinet rank in Canada. The Territorial "Parliament" and administrative buildings could perhaps easily have been replaced for $50,000. They served all useful purposes, however, and housed a large and very busy staff. Sir Frederick Haultain, now Chief Justice of Saskatchewan, was Premier and his solitary colleague was Hon. James Ross, now a member of the Senate. Each looked after three portfolios. It was a "coalition" Government. Each department was presided over by a permanent deputy head, who had an absolutely free hand in regard to staff appointments and dismissals, and was held strictly responsible for results. The Hon. James Calder, now Federal Minister of Immigration, was deputy of the Educational Department. Col. J.S. Dennis, [now] Assistant to the President, C.P.R., was in charge of Public Works; J.A. Reid, until recently Alberta's capable Agent General in Great Britain, looked after the Treasury and two other minor departments, and the writer was deputy head of the Agriculture Department. This was an out and out "business" administration. One never observed the slightest indication of "playing politics." The two new Provinces created from these territories were started practically without a dollar of public debt, on autonomy being granted. Look at their financial position today!

◆

It is to be noted that when the United States seceded from Britain and drafted its own constitution, it did not adopt holus-bolus the form of government which then existed in Great Britain. Perhaps Uncle Sam was wise in his generation.

When a new President is elected in the United States he invites to his Cabinet the most outstanding personalities in the country. Each is selected with a view to his special fitness for the department he is to administer. While the President may not always exercise exceptional judgment, and while party considerations may, and frequently do, dictate nominations, yet there cannot be the least doubt that on the whole, the cabinet material of that country is generally of the very highest order. The President has the whole country to select from.

In Canada, on the contrary, the system works quite differently. Let us suppose that a General Election returns the opposition party to power, with a workable majority. The leader is thereupon requested by the King's representative to form a government. The first obstacle to intelligent selection that meets the new Prime Minister, who is, of course, practically restricted, in his selection, to the elected members of Parliament, is territorial claims. The unwritten law is that each Province must have so many cabinet representatives. Next comes the fact that a certain number of these cabinet representatives must, if possible, be French-speaking. Then come religious considerations. An undue preponderance of Methodists, Presbyterians or Roman Catholics could not, for a moment, be countenanced.

There is scarcely ever a government formed that does not include several members who find themselves within the charmed circle purely by force of circumstances. Men, who, in private life, probably would not be entrusted with the responsibility of managing the smallest kind of business, are pitchforked into the administration of important public departments. Every possible consideration, except that of efficiency, governs in the construction of Dominion cabinet. If Canada is ever to enjoy efficient "business" Government, it is quite evident that local jealousies must be eliminated so as to leave to the Prime Minister, at least, the meagre privilege of selecting from amongst his entire following in Parliament the best talent that may be available, irrespective of creed, race or territorial considerations.

But it is perhaps unfair to expect too much, from our Federal Ministers, at any rate. Just think of the salaries we pay! The Prime Minister of Canada receives the pay of the manager of a fairly important branch bank in Canada.

———————◆———————

Our Civil Services, provincial and federal, are on an entirely wrong basis. An effort has been made by the Dominion authorities to abolish patronage by creating a Civil Service Commission. In most of the Provinces the "spoils" system is frankly in vogue. It is doubtful whether appointments by a commission will result in personnel much superior to the old patronage system, i.e., nomination by members of Parliament.

How would a great business concern handle this question? The head would appoint his principal executives, the executives their staffs, and so on all the way down. A chain of responsibility would thus be established from the bottom up. Our great railway organizations, with many times the number of employees our Governments have, are built on this plan. The president of the company appoints his general manager. The latter selects his superintendents, who in turn exercise control over the roadmasters, who appoint the section foremen, who hire and fire the maintenance-of-way men under them. It is a system of rigid responsibility of bosses, for the work and actions of their subordinates.

Is there any reason why a deputy head of a public department, selected by the responsible minister, should not be responsible for the appointment of his chief lieutenants and each of these in turn appoint or nominate the subordinates in his own branch or bureau? We could then hold our men responsible for results, which we cannot do now. This would be sound organization.

There also seems to be a superstition abroad, and I feel bound to say that it is not confined to Canada, that once a person enters the public service of his country he is provided for during life. It is precisely this security of tenure idea that destroys the morale of our Civil Service.

The present Civil Service Commission has done excellent work and could, under the system suggested, render still more valuable services. It should remain the clearing house and receive all applications for employment, including those submitted through members of Parliament. It should occupy the front trenches against any attack by patronage hunters and would be a Government employment bureau to which the various responsible officials would apply for such help as was needed. But the appointment would be made by the responsible officer and not by the Commission. It could also deal with cases of complaint of wrongful dismissal. It could assist in improving the service in a hundred ways, especially with respect to economy and efficiency. It should have complete power of investigation into office organization in any department of the service and should have on its staff efficiency experts in various lines. It should interest itself in promoting standard office routine and practice throughout the entire service.

———————◆———————

During the period of the War, the Federal Government deemed it necessary to create various boards and commissions to administer certain new and special war services. It became fashionable amongst a certain class of newspapers and public speakers to cast ridicule on this new development in administration. The phrase "government by commission" was coined and worked to death. One often wonders whether these self-appointed critics ever gave a moment's serious thought to the matter.

When the war came, the Government wisely recognized the impossibility of properly performing, directly, the many new functions forced upon it by exigencies of war, and, therefore, resorted to the commission expedient. The experiment proved satisfactory. Some of these war institutions, notably the War Purchasing Commission, did such successful work and effected such striking economies that they are now to be merged in the permanent establishment at Ottawa in their present, or a slightly modified, form.

As a general proposition, and having in view efficiency, the various Governments throughout Canada might well study the success of these Federal administrative war commissions. The great spending departments of the Government, such as the Post Office and Public Works Departments, should be administered by a small executive board or commission, including the chief officers of each department, possibly presided over by the responsible Minister. This principle has now been recognized as sound by the amalgamation of Government railways under the management of a board of directors nominated by the Government.

Can any argument be advanced against the elimination of partisan politics from the Post Office management, for instance? Will anyone deny that ten per cent of the post offices and mail routes in Canada are absolutely unnecessary, that the Minister is importuned by local members for new offices and other favours day in and day out, that, in fact, under capable management, the really beneficial services of the department could be vastly improved and the annual deficit be transformed into a surplus?

A new minister comes in. He is imbued with progressive ideas. His administration shall be a red letter period in Canada's postal administration. "Penny postage" is the thing. The letter rate is reduced and followed by further post-office deficits. But this minister is heralded as a public benefactor. Of course, it is all for personal glorification and political effect. And the joke of it is that the man on the street fails to be impressed. The man on the farm laughs at it all. How many letters does he write in a year? Does not the entire benefit of the reform almost exclusively affect the big mail-order establishments, financial institutions, and other interests that largely use the mail services of the country? Would a business board endorse any such foolish, revenue-destroying proposal as that?

◆

Canada's imitation House of Lords, our national "Divorce Mill," is perhaps the most pathetically inefficient and impotent branch of our representative system. While the House of Lords at Westminster has been described as the most brilliant aggregation of legislators in the world, and, while the Senate of the United States has arrogated to itself the supreme position in the administration of that country, Canada's Senate has generally been ineffective and mediocre. When, in the political history of the country, it has been called upon to be gloriously patriotic, it has only been partisan. Whatever the Upper Chamber was intended to do has surely never been done, as one can credit scarcely a single great action to this fifth wheel of our legislative machinery. It is supposed to serve as a check on ill-considered, ill-digested legislation. It does not fulfil that function. If it did, its life would probably be short, because the country would not tamely submit to gravely electing its popular representatives merely to have their acts nullified by a wholly irresponsible body.

The British North America Act 1867 provided for the appointment of 24 senators each for Quebec and Ontario and the same for the Maritime Provinces. Why 24 and not 48, or any other arbitrary number has never been explained. Other portions of Canada have necessarily had to be dealt with, by way of amendment to the Act, from time to time. This is another bright and shining example of the delightfully promiscuous methods of our Fathers of Confederation. There was evidently no definite purpose or plan to be served in making provisions for Canada's Upper Chamber. In the United States, there are two senators representing each political unit. Nevada, with less than a hundred thousand people, has precisely the same Senate representation as New York with over nine millions. The Senate there is evidently designed to protect the interests of the smaller States and less densely populated sections of the Union. This is a definite and clear-cut mission.

It is not difficult to trace the causes of the generally un-satisfactory status of Canada's Senate. The vicious practice of making the Senate a convenient vehicle for bestowing rewards upon useful and importunate party-hacks, and making it the dumping-ground for mediocre politicians rejected at the polls, has something to do with it. This flagrant prostitution of a legislative body that surely must have been intended to fulfil important duties, functioning in an atmosphere removed from partisan and other sordid influences, has evidently brought in its train the inevitable result—public contempt and dry-rot. Such a body obviously cannot rise above its personnel, and the responsibility for this lies with past and present Governments.

That the Senate should be frankly partisan in its attitude towards legislation submitted to it, now seems to be accepted as a matter of course. Yet, a moment's reflection should make it clear that this is precisely what the Senate should never be, under any circumstances whatever. The mere suspicion of partisanship destroys the last shred of its usefulness and justification in the public estimation. A partisan senator should be placed in the same category as a partisan judge—an object of scorn and contempt.

A popular grievance against the Senate is its tender solicitude for the welfare of the "interests." Perhaps this is partly accounted for by the fact that out of its complement of 93 members, there are 23 lawyers, and 60 representatives of other professions, commerce and industry. The interests of agriculture are championed by 9 farmers and labour has one whole undivided representative all to herself!

If we are to maintain an expensive institution like the Senate, arrangements ought certainly to be made to give it useful work to do and to put a check on the appointments. As a first step, in connection with all nominations to the Senate, provision might very well be made compelling the government of the day to submit to Parliament the name of the proposed appointee, with a complete record of the public services he has performed, and a statement of the special qualifications that caused the Government to recommend him as a useful addition to the Upper House. Provision should also be made for the retirement of Senators upon reaching an advanced age. Compulsory attendance at all sessions of the Senate, or evidence of physical inability to attend, should likewise be insisted upon, and absence for a certain length of time should automatically render the seat vacant. These reforms would be better than the present intolerable situation.

FIVE

Public Administration of Commerce and Industry

IT CANNOT BE DENIED that as an educational factor, political and social, the Great War occupies the centre of the stage. During the past four years we have been taught many illuminating lessons, the most striking of all being perhaps the facility with which the State stepped in, all over the world, and calmly took possession of mines, great industries, steamships and railways. It organized huge trading concerns, wrote insurance by the billion, in fact, did precisely all the things that our reactionaries have sedulously been telling us could never be done by the State. Vested interests were swept to one side over-night, and State control came into being, and the evidence now available seems to be that the latter, on the whole, proved very successful.

All this happened under war conditions, and it is not perhaps fair to draw too rigid conclusions from the special experiences of war-time. One important factor in favour of success was undoubtedly that all petty, partisan criticisms were silenced during the great crisis, thus giving governments a freer hand; also that outstanding men, who, under ordinary circumstances, could not be secured for public employment, were available for responsible positions. But the fact remains that this thing has been done, and successfully, and the "man on the street" is therefore, not as timid in discussing the policy of public ownership and administration, as he was once upon a time. The chances are that a sufficient number of people may even be induced to vote for it one of these days, when the "powers that be" will be confronted with the problem as a practical proposition.

In the earlier forms of civilization the only public responsibility undertaken was to organize the nation to repel attacks from the outside and thus enable the people to pursue their callings in peace. As civilization progressed and became more complicated, the State found it necessary to interest itself more closely in the life of the individual citizen in many ways. Today the State performs an enormous amount of what is properly called welfare work. Health, sanitation, education, the protection of life and property, etc., are all regarded as legitimate state enterprises. The individualistic attitude is vanishing. The "new spirit" is abroad, and it is difficult to forecast what new activities in the way of public enterprise the not distant future may have in store for us.

It is usual at socialist and Bolshevist meetings in Canada to denounce the "interests" and to demand Government ownership and operation of this, that and the other utility and industry. The issue is distinctly before the country and the disciples of Karl Marx will see to it that it remains there. Under the circumstances, it is in order to examine the proposal judicially and fairly. It is, judging by past standards, an extraordinary and unusual proposition, but we must train our minds to get used to these unusual proposals. They are here to stay.

We hear a great deal of criticism in connection with the organization of "big business," and not entirely without good reason. Big business, however, is not necessarily bad business or corrupt business. In the amalgamation of industrial concerns, banks, railways, etc., vast economies are generally effected, which, under public-spirited management, would benefit the consumer in the way of lower prices. The actual effect has, however, generally been exactly the reverse. With the elimination of competition, prices have often, not always, been increased. These mergers have also been made the excuse for the inflation of capital for which the consumer is asked to provide dividends. This perhaps is the most objectionable feature of such transactions and is dealt with elsewhere. In

the United States the Sherman Act has put a stop to such operations. Those who believe in public ownership may, however,
derive some comfort from the fact that the creation of mergers is a
very valuable contribution towards the cause they espouse. The
merger has been well characterized as the "halfway house to public
ownership." Obviously the State or the municipality can much
more readily take over a well organized monopolistic industry than
a vast number of smaller concerns acting independently. Therefore,
let the good work proceed—but control the merger, as far as possible.

It is universally conceded that the principle of co-operation is
sound. Co-operative business has made enormous strides in many
European countries and in some of the overseas colonies. We have
outstanding examples of successful cohesive effort in organized
business in Canada. The Grain Growers' movement in the West is a
case in point. We must also take into consideration the indisputable
fact that the first step in civilization was the co-ordination of energy
and the banding together of human beings for co-operative effort in
mutual aid. Every advance in social and individual growth may be
traced to cohesive organization. Public administration of business
and industry is merely a step in the evolution of the co-operative
principle. In fact, it is its logical goal.

On looking back a few decades, one is impressed with the fact
that the tendency in Canada has been distinctly toward public ownership of utilities. Urban centres which had granted franchises for
water supply, lighting, surface transportation, etc., have gradually,
on the expiration of these monopolies, gathered them into their
own municipal organizations and, on the whole, efficiency and
economy have been fairly well observed in the administration of
such utilities. The cases of glaring failure have probably not been
much more numerous than they would have been under private or
corporate ownership. In other words, the experiment has been reasonably encouraging up to date. If, here and there, money has been
lost on operation, the chances are that the citizens have benefited in
better service than they would have received under private control.

The following are the four main questions to be examined in re-

gard to the feasibility of a general policy of public administration of
commerce and industry:

1. Are we far enough advanced socially and educationally to
   eliminate the element of competition from our industrial and
   commercial system?
2. Can the Government operate as economically and efficiently
   as private enterprise?
3. Will the public prove to be a better and more generous employer than private enterprise?
4. What would be the political effect of widespread public administration?

There are very grave reasons for approaching the subject with
great caution and a realization that much new ground may have to
be broken before Canada can safely tread the paths of advanced socialism.

◆

The most outstanding effect of public administration would be the
elimination of competition and of private gain. The term "public
administration" would, of course, include Federal, Provincial, and
Municipal management of business. At first sight, and to our very
limited vision, the proposal is staggering, but on closer study it will
be found to be in line with human progress generally. It is dangerous to set up private industry as a thing sacred and inviolate. We
should realize that industry carried out on the present enormous
scale, and under the factory system, is of comparatively modern origin. Our old people will remember a very different organization of
industry. It might, therefore, with perfect propriety be held that the
factory system, coupled with private or corporate ownership, is just
on trial and is as yet in the experimental stage. Considerations of
public interest will ultimately govern the policy to be followed.

Our competitive system unquestionably rests upon a reasonably
sound foundation. Smiles says

Competition... is [said to be]: "heartless," "selfish," "mischie-
vous," "ruinous" and so on. It is said to produce misery and
poverty to the millions.

And yet there is something to be said for competition, as well as against it. It is a struggle—that must be admitted. All life is a struggle. Among workmen, competition is a struggle to advance toward higher wages. Among masters, to make the highest profits. Among writers, preachers and politicians, it is a struggle to succeed—to gain glory, reputation or income. Like everything human, it has a mixture of evil in it. If one man prospers more than others, or if some classes of men prosper more than others, they leave other classes of men behind them. Not that they leave those others worse, but that they themselves advance.

Put a stop to competition and you merely check the progress of individuals and of classes. You preserve a dead uniform level. You stereotype society and its several orders and conditions. The motive for emulation is taken away and caste, with all its mischiefs, is perpetuated. Stop competition, and you stop the struggle of individualism. You also stop the advancement of individualism and, through that, of society at large.

Under competition, the lazy man is put under the necessity of exerting himself; and if he will not exert himself, he must fall behind. If he does not work, neither shall he eat. My lazy friend, you must not look to me to do my share of the world's work and yours too! You must do your own fair share of work, save your own money, and not look to me and to others to keep you out of the poorhouse. There is enough for all; but do your own share of work you must.

Success grows out of struggles to overcome difficulties. If there were no difficulties, there would be no success. If there were nothing to struggle or compete for, there would be nothing achieved. It is well, therefore, that men should be under the necessity of exerting themselves. In this necessity for exertion we find the chief source of human advancement—the advancement of individuals as of nations. It has led to most of the splendid mechanical inventions and improvements of the age. It has stimulated the ship-builder, the merchant, the manufacturer, the machinist, the tradesman, the skilled workman. In all departments of productive industry, it has been the moving power. It has developed the resources of this and other countries—the resources of the soil, and the character and qualities of the men who dwell upon it. It seems to be absolutely necessary for the purpose of stimulating the growth and culture of every individual. It is deeply rooted in man, leading him ever to seek after, and endeavour to realize, something better and higher than he has yet attained. . . .

I could wish that every impatient reformer would learn this by heart and ask himself honestly whether our social state is sufficiently far advanced to eliminate the impulse of competition from our daily lives and efforts. Much water will run under the bridges before the sense of duty to the public is sufficiently strongly developed, even in the majority of men, to justify our country in embarking upon any wide policy that would ignore the driving power of competition.

Our labour organizations today are, in a measure, endeavouring to minimize the effect of the competitive system by means of the standard wage. But, on the other hand, no trade union man would for a moment subscribe to the principle that the hodcarrier should receive the same pay as the bricklayer, or the labourer as the plumber. Such being the case, the principle must also be accepted that the foreman must receive higher pay than those below him and the competent manager still higher. All of which is tantamount to admitting that human beings are cast in various moulds, that the value of their services consequently varies enormously, and that this principle applies even within the same occupations. It also becomes clear that no cast-iron rules that eliminate the personal equation can be enforced with justice. Some one, in fact, must determine the value of the services of each individual and this value, in turn, depends largely on the amount of competition there is for such services. The consistent socialist evidently has obstacles to surmount, and, possibly, sacrifices to make, before the world can accept his creed of equality!

The great majority of those who believe in public administration of enterprise would confine such activities to utilities and perhaps certain selected industries and business enterprises that would readily lend themselves to consolidation under State or municipal management.

Before private enterprise, spurred into vigorous and daring action by the hope of ultimate success and its legitimate reward, can be entirely ignored as a factor in our scheme of national life, a new and superior race of men and women, with higher ideals and aspirations, patiently inculcated through generations of high thinking and plain living, must take the places of the modern frail and selfish human animals. That seems reasonably clear.

◆

A very important argument in favor of public administration lies in the facility with which capital can be thereby obtained for all legitimate purposes and the low rate of interest at which it can be employed. This is, of course, an enormous advantage if properly utilized and if other things are equal. Private or corporate ownership cannot begin to compete in this respect. Another asset is the ability of the public to create a monopoly, absolute or virtual, and, therefore, to absorb all the business available in any particular line.

In all successful enterprise, the direction and inspiration come from the top. It centres ultimately in one single individual who has the capacity and imagination to organize, direct and inspire his subordinates. Such an individual commands a high rate of remuneration. He furnishes the brains and driving power of all successful undertakings. The competition for his services is keen. He possesses, perhaps, the most valuable business qualification with which any human being can be endowed. He is seldom in public employment. The price offered is not high enough and the conditions of employment are unsatisfactory and generally distasteful.

Strange as it may appear, one of the main problems of public administration is making it possible to induce this type of man to accept public service. He knows his own value. He is not a political log-roller or ward-heeler. He will not put up with the ignorant and vicious criticism or interference of the butcher-alderman or the backwoods lawyer, who has successfully broken into politics, any more than he would stand for similar tactics from an over-fed capitalist or pompous director under private or corporate employment. Neither has he any intention whatever of being hounded by or being made the innocent victim of partisan attacks on the administration of the day, Federal, Provincial or Municipal, by sensational newspapers whose one mission in life is to throw discredit on the "ins" to the advantage of the "outs." The type of man under discussion jealously guards his reputation. It is his stock-in-trade. He cannot afford to jeopardize it through having his name dragged in the mud in the interest of partisan politics. And this is generally the ultimate fate of professional men who manage public utilities today.

Quite incidentally, the failure of advanced socialism to recognize in its scheme of reorganization of industry and business the vital and outstanding position of the type of man referred to, stamps the whole system as unworkable.

The complete disregard by our modern socialist of the supreme importance of skilled management in industry is almost pathetic. It is painfully clear that socialistic doctrines need revision very badly in the light of the experiences of recent years and the dictates of common business sense. However important capital and labour may fancy themselves to be, the most important element in successful industry is management.

Another serious drawback to public ownership and operation, even of utilities, is the general lack of intelligence and absence of clear thinking on the part of the average ratepayer. He finds it hard to understand the necessity for scrapping obsolete machinery before it is worn out, or for making capital expenditure on buildings and equipment to cheapen production and service. Municipal authorities cannot afford experimentation. They are too timid to take the ten per cent chance of failure that private enterprise cheerfully assumes in working out an expensive problem that promises results. This attitude leads to stagnation in management and kills enterprise absolutely. No business can succeed conspicuously under such conditions.

◆

The question of the position of labour under public administration is worthy of most serious thought on the part of labour organizations. There are a great many points from which the question must be considered. If the public is the ideal employer and paymaster, as the advanced school of socialism claims, it, of course, follows that the fullest and most impartial justice will be meted out to labour in public employment. Facts, however, do not appear to justify this view.

The Government of Canada, for instance, is notoriously the meanest skinflint among employers. How the Federal authorities are able to retain the services of the multitude of highly skilled and capable men in the public service, is a mystery to me. In considering the lower grades of Federal employees, one is at once struck by the meagre wages of postmen, messengers, etc. Could anything be more wretched? The Provincial Governments are little better. In the face of an enormously increasing cost of living during recent years, salaries and wages have been practically stationary. Any slight advances or bonuses that have been asked by employees have been resisted by every possible means and, finally, grudgingly conceded. The present condition is decidedly a most discouraging state of affairs from the point of view of labour's interests under public administration.

The municipality as an employer is worthy of more than passing remark, as, under any scheme of public operation, it is evident that the municipality must play by far the most prominent part. Public utilities are now operated under municipal auspices all over Canada and we have, therefore, actual performance to guide us in our inquiry, apart from conclusions based on theory only.

The first astounding fact that greets the investigators is that strikes of municipal employees have occurred frequently in various parts of Canada. Now, one can scarcely reconcile the right to strike, with public employment, nor is it logical for labour so engaged to use the offensive measures apparently found necessary in dealing with irresponsible private employers. If the public is the ideal employer, coercive action cannot be justified. If not, labour must evidently revise its views on public administration. There seems no other alternative.

The last, but not least, important phase of public administration of business and industry is now to be considered, namely, the political effect of any widespread adoption of such a policy by the Federal or Provincial Government. An army of Government employees would be distributed throughout the country. In fact, the policy carried out in its entirety would mean that a very large proportion of the urban adult population of Canada would owe its living directly to the Government. Such a state of affairs would present some interesting problems.

Each disgruntled employee would, of course, vote against the Government in a spirit of revenge or reprisal. The great majority of public servants would probably vote in favour of the Government of the day, out of loyalty. In both cases the motive behind the vote would be a highly improper one for a model democracy and would fail to convey a fair expression of opinion on the general record of the Government. Such a vastly important section of the vote would in nearly all cases swing the whole election.

One can almost visualize, on the eve of a general election, the efforts of the practical statesman, whose tenure of office depends upon a satisfied public service, and of the opposition element, striving to attain office. Each would go one better than the other, in the way of salaries, working hours, and pensions. The public servant would indeed be in an enviable position. Instead of working for the public, the public would work for him!

There would also be a great danger of creating an absolutely irresponsible bureaucracy.

SIX

Our Transportation Problems

GREAT BRITAIN, IN developing the most inefficient transportation system on earth, unwittingly rendered services of incalculable value to her overseas dominions. They all profited by the horrible example—that is, all but Canada. In some cases, freight rates in England on privately owned railways are ten times as large as the rates on Government operated lines on the Continent of Europe. You can ship frozen meats from New Zealand to a British port at one-half the cost of shipping British meat to the same port from another county in England. British agriculture has been strangled and destroyed under the blighting influence of its railway system. The canal system of England has been almost completely absorbed by the railway interests and competition thus eliminated. Parliament is impotent. It is said that twenty per cent of the members of the British House of Commons are directors of British railways and the majority of the members own railway shares or bonds. Every effort at reform is stifled at birth. In Canada, undoubtedly, political rather than business considerations have in the past dictated our railway policies and we have thus succeeded in imposing upon this young country staggering burdens which must remain to impede our progress for generations to come. Ordinary intelligence also seems to have been lacking in some of the decisions reached and measures taken. We have proceeded on our way like a ship without a rudder in charge of a drunken pilot!

◆

Canada now has a Railway Commission clothed with the most complete and arbitrary powers. No railway can advance rates without its formal consent. If any community deems itself discriminated against in rates or service, its case can be brought before this body, which will hear the evidence on both sides and render and enforce a decision. This constitutes complete control and eliminates practically the value of competition altogether. Rates all over Canada, passenger and freight, are standard. Ten railways or one, they remain the same for all. Our whole and sole interest in railways, therefore, reduces itself absolutely to economical and efficient operations, so that rates may be reduced to, or kept at, the lowest possible level and the cost of living thereby prevented from increasing. Obviously, the greater the business any individual line controls, the more economically the traffic can be handled, and the lower the rates would necessarily be under our system of control. The more competition there is for a certain volume of traffic and the more roads share in it, quite clearly, the higher the cost per ton per mile and, consequently, the higher the rate the public must pay, and the higher the cost of living becomes.

We should never have permitted the railway service of Canada to pass into the hands of private corporations. Canada's railway system should, in the first place, have been planned with a single eye to efficiency and economy in operation. Instead of several parallel lines into our great cities we would then have had one standard, double-track, or fourtrack, trunk line, capable of handling the entire business available, at the lowest cost. This was the greatest service Government ownership could ever have rendered Canada. But this splendid opportunity was, in the earlier history of the Dominion, recklessly dissipated by unscrupulous politicians and incapable administrators. Now we must perforce lie on the bed we have ourselves made.

◆

Purely as a matter of interesting speculation, and in order to bring home to Canadians the extreme danger of the *laisser faire* attitude in regard to the railway policies of the country and general administration, it is useful to give a bird's eye view of the result of our past policy of subsidizing the construction of railways by private interest. The Drayton-Ackworth report contains the following statement showing the cost to the country of Government lines and also the aid given other systems by the Government of Canada:

	Subsidies	Proceeds of lands sold	Loans outstanding or investment	Guarantees outstanding	Total
	$	$	$	$	$
Canadian Northern	38,874,148	34,379,809	25,858,166	199,141,140	298,253,263
Canadian Pacific	104,690,801	123,810,124			228,500,925
Grand Trunk Railway	13,003,060		15,142,633		28,145,693
Grand Trunk Pacific	726,320		70,311,716	43,432,848	114,470,884
Grand Trunk Pacific Branch Lines				13,469,004	13,469,004
National Transcontinental			159,881,197		159,881,197
Intercolonial			116,234,204		116,234,204
Prince Edward Island			9,496,567		9,496,567
Total	157,294,329	158,189,933	396,924,483	256,042,992	968,451,737

Under subsidies to the Canadian Pacific Railway has been included the estimated cost of construction east of Winnipeg handed over to that company by the Government. The report goes on to say:

... Not counting the loss of interest for many years upon the investment in roads operated by the Government, it appears that for the eight systems, in which the public is most interested, the people of Canada, through their Governments, have provided, or guaranteed, the payment of sums totalling $968,451,737. This works out at over $30,000 per mile of road. But even this is not all. In addition, they have granted great areas of land as yet unsold and unpledged. They have undertaken the construction of other lines whose cost will be an important addition to this large outlay. Further, in the case of some of the companies included above, to which they have given or lent large sums of money to meet pressing needs, unlike private lenders, who would naturally have demanded a security charged in front of all previous investment, they have voluntarily accepted a charge ranking after the bulk of the private capital already put into the undertaking. . . .

When will the people of Canada "wake up" and take an intelligent interest in the business management of the country? Here we have the appalling spectacle of seven hundred millions of dollars of cash and land donations, and contingent liability incurred, to provide necessary railway communication, while the State has not at this moment one dollar's worth of assets to show in return! There cannot be the least doubt that if, early in our history, our Governments had planned a single railway trunk system for Canada, with provision for extensions as required, the entire cost could have been met out of this amount, and the country would today be the owner of all its railways without further liability. Above everything, there would be no operating problem to meet. The undertaking would be on a paying basis unless strangled by mismanagement. Our childlike faith in our statesmen has been sublime.

◆

Canada's agricultural West is hemmed in on the East by a thousand miles of wilderness and on the West by another few hundred miles of the same character of country, the Rocky Mountains. We cannot hope for cheaper transportation in either direction. It is an unpleasant prospect. Our no-man's-land is now a perpetual tax on the people of the West and to some extent on the East as well. It is the key to the transportation situation in Canada.

◆

During recent years two more lines, the Canadian Northern and the National Transcontinental, have been chartered and built through the same territory and at enormous public expense. Both have, of course, failed miserably and are now on the hands of an over-enthusiastic State, and present a problem that almost defies human ingenuity in unravelling and administering so as not to involve the absolute abandonment of millions of dollars of capital expenditure. That such will ultimately be found expedient, few rational people doubt at this time.

It is refreshing to recall that when the charter of the National Transcontinental came before Parliament, Sir Robert Borden, at that time leader of the Opposition, advanced the suggestion that the Canadian Pacific line between Winnipeg and North Bay should be nationalized and improved, and all roads given running rights over it. This, of course, was the rational step for Canada to have taken, but the suggestion, emanating from the Opposition, could not be accepted. It would have looked too much like business methods. So it was promptly ridiculed by the Government of the day, and speaker after speaker dwelt on the enormous development that was to take place in the West, and predicted that the traffic available would soon be beyond the power of all three lines to cope with. And thus were fastened on Canada's wrists the manacles that will be there for generations after the amateur railway builders of that period have joined their forefathers.

———————◆———————

For many years there has been an agitation in the West for an outlet to Hudson's Bay for agricultural products, chiefly grain. On the map, such a plan looks attractive, but time and again, the route has been investigated by fairly competent authority, and has been uniformly condemned. I cannot do better than quote the summing up of the Royal Commission on Railways and Transportation on this subject:

.... We understand that construction work on the Hudson Bay line has been suspended. We think that the work should not in any case be recommenced till more urgent needs have been met, and money is more easily procurable. And if the work on the line is begun again, we think it should be done in the most economical manner possible, and only up to the standard of a local line, bearing in mind that it cannot be expected for many years to come to be self-supporting. Considering the small advantage in rail mileage from the grain-growing areas, which the Hudson Bay possesses over the existing routes to Port Arthur, and that from many districts it possesses no advantage at all; considering further the short and uncertain period of navigation in the bay, and that grain consigned to Port Nelson will consequently always be liable to be detained there for nine months till navigation is again opened; considering that higher ocean freights may be expected to absorb, if not more than absorb, any possible saving in rail rates, we cannot believe that this route will ever secure any serious share in the export trade. Still less can we think that it will handle an import business. Unless considerable mineral wealth should be discovered in the territory which this line will open up, it must, we fear, continue to be almost indefinitely a burden upon the people of Canada. And everything that can be done should be done to make this burden as small as possible. . . .

It was recently stated in Parliament that some twenty million dollars has now been spent on this undertaking. Over six million dollars has gone on terminals at Port Nelson. Canada has thus one more white elephant on her hands.

I have no cut and dried remedy to offer for such a dangerous state of affairs. That it is the product of sheer ignorance is clear. Why should it be possible for any small group of men, probably lacking outstanding business ability, to pledge the country to purposeless expenditure of millions of dollars merely to satisfy the importunate demands of a class of citizens badly informed on the subject of the proposed expenditure? It is entirely wrong.

◆

The capitalization per mile of the lines now included in the new system is illuminating. The Intercolonial embracing 1,941 miles of lines is capitalized at $71,000 per mile. If interest is included, which it should be, the capitalization would be over $100,000 per mile.

The National Transcontinental, comprising 1,811 miles of railway, was a veritable sink-hole for public funds. It represents actual expenditure of $92,000 per mile and, with interest charges capitalized, stands the country at approximately $113,000 per mile.

The Canadian Northern system was, on the whole, very economically built, although considerable further expenditure will be needed to bring it up to standard. It cost the country a total of about $45,000 per mile, including interest charges, and embraces somewhat under 10,000 miles of line.

The Grand Trunk Pacific was also a very costly undertaking, though well built. It includes 1,748 miles of lines, which, with the rolling stock, cost over $100,000 per mile.

There can be no reasonable doubt that the proposed amalgamated national railway system will start business, in point of gross earning power, not very far in advance of where the Canadian Pacific was thirty or more years ago. It will labour under all kinds of handicaps, some of them subject to solution, whilst others will remain as a millstone around its neck. An enormous capital cost has been piled up against these lines and fixed charges per mile will probably be soaring high above anything hitherto known in transportation in new countries.

Here we are at once confronted with a difficulty. While the National system must have higher rates to pay even its bare operating and maintenance expenses, the Canadian Pacific is able to render precisely the same services at a much lower cost and still pay a satisfactory dividend to its shareholders, and therefore, does not require increases rates. But, obviously, rate increases cannot be made effective on the National system without also extending them to the Canadian Pacific, or everything would be routed over the latter and the National system would have no traffic. We, therefore, clearly perceive that the introduction of competition in railway transportation in Canada has actually had the direct effect of enormously increasing our freight rates.

When the final general rate increase took place in the latter part of 1918, the Government saw this problem. Rates had to be enormously advanced; or all the lines comprised, or to be comprised, in the National system, would go bankrupt. The Canadian

Pacific, on the other hand, being able to carry on without any considerable advance in rates, a bargain was made whereby, in consideration of a twenty-five per cent increase in freight rates being granted, the Canadian Pacific would submit to special taxation to enable the Government to collect, for the benefit of the public, a certain part of its surplus earnings.

———————◆———————

The United States Government took over the railways on an agreement to compensate the shareholders on a basis of the average net earnings for the three pre-war years. February, 1919 falls short 37 million dollars of meeting this guarantee. January of the same year produced a deficit of 55 million dollars!

This unfavourable showing is not primarily due to inefficiency in operation, although competent authorities claim that State management is not sufficiently elastic in promptly reducing staff and other expenses in slack periods. The important factor, however, is increased labour cost. The Government has advanced wages by approximately one billion dollars per annum since taking control. The American railway worker has, since 1915, had his annual wages increased from an average of $800 to an average of $1,400. To offset this, passenger rates have been increased 50 per cent and freight rates 25 per cent, which was estimated to produce sufficient revenue. This apparently it has failed to do so far.

Turning to Great Britain, we find the situation frankly desperate. The disturbing factor there has, of course, been the impossibility of increasing the staggering pre-war freight rates without creating a condition where the entire traffic of the country would revert to the ancient highways and the railways be left idle and bankrupt. Railway capital in Great Britain has for some years been on a 4 per cent earning basis and the lines were taken over by the Government on a guarantee of this earning. The annual gross earnings have been 680 million dollars, wages 250 millions, taxes 25 millions and materials 155 millions, leaving net earnings to shareholders 250 million dollars per annum.

The British railway worker had been on an average annual wage of $350. The Government was quickly confronted with a demand for increases which could not be compensated by transferring the burden to the public. Railway workers there have now received eight separate increases, bringing the average per man up to $900 and adding 400 million dollars to the annual operating cost. To this, increases in cost of materials have added another 140 million dollars. The annual pay-roll now is 650 millions. Including the 4 per cent rental, it now costs the Government yearly 1,220 million dollars to operate the railways—an increase of 80 per cent over pre-war days—and taking into account the 50 per cent increase in passenger rates, the total gross revenue is only 780 million dollars. The estimated annual deficit is thus 440 million dollars! There is, of course, only one way out of this muddle, namely, for the State to take over the railways and pass the burden on to the people by means of general taxation. It cannot be done by increasing freight rates.

In Canada we have had three general freight rate increases; in 1916 about 5 per cent, 15 per cent in March, 1918, and 25 per cent during the following August, making a total advance over the pre-war standard of slightly over fifty per cent. It is significant that when the various freight rate advances were announced in Canada comparatively little public comment was caused. It was, of course, generally considered a regrettable, though unavoidable, incident and the situation was philosophically dismissed with a patient shrug of the shoulder and public attention was soon diverted to more interesting and impressive domestic affairs—such, for instance, as the latest baseball news and the state of the golf course. The attitude of the "man on the street" on these occasions demonstrated strikingly his extraordinary apathy towards the vital issues facing his country. Needless to say, these rate decisions were among the most momentous events in Canada's history. *They brought into effect the heaviest tax ever imposed on the people of this country.*

The Government of Canada authorized a 50 per cent increase of freight rates and approximately a 15 per cent increase in passenger rates on all railways. The immediate effect of this ruling was, of course, that a consumption tax was automatically levied on the people of Canada amounting to about 118 million dollars per annum—exceeding by nearly thirty million dollars our normal annual import tax revenue and coming within forty million dollars of equalling the entire taxation revenue of Canada from all sources in the most prosperous year the country ever witnessed! Quite incidentally, the bare suggestion of reducing Canada's present protective tariff is met with the hysterical shriek: "Where is our revenue going to come from?" We are apparently unable to comprehend how we can partly convert a consumption tax of a round hundred millions into a direct tax of the same dimensions without becoming bankrupt. But we see no obstacle whatever to levying over night an entirely new additional consumption tax of 118 millions! We "strain at a gnat and swallow a camel." The Canadian taxpayer is either a most inconsistent individual or, surely, we are rapidly losing our sense of proportion.

Canada's railway situation is, of course, largely controlled by that of the United States. Increases in wages on the railways there are almost automatically duplicated in Canada. In studying the record of State operation of railways in Great Britain and across the line, the fact stands out prominently and clearly that the one item of wage cost has been chiefly responsible for the disastrous results up to date.

———————◆———————

The obvious course to pursue is to inaugurate a well conceived and energetic colonization policy. Unfortunately, most of the vacant lands along the Canadian Northern and Grand Trunk Pacific in the West are owned by the Canadian Pacific Railway, the nation's only competitor in transportation. This company is naturally interested in attracting settlement to its own system and perhaps is not over-enthusiastic in assisting in the creation of traffic for the National lines and may, therefore, prove somewhat unsympathetic.

The Canadian Northern location in the West is tributary to what is perhaps the best part of that country. In time it will be a gold mine in the way of traffic. The Grand Trunk Pacific is not, however, in the same fortunate position. It traverses much inferior country, but may be expected to yield fair traffic returns as development takes place. The Canadian Pacific taps the main wheat producing areas of Saskatchewan and Alberta and will probably always command the greater freight tonnage. The country served by the National system, being largely covered with poplar and, therefore, inclined to produce a softer wheat, will be settled chiefly by smaller land-holders, who will specialize in dairying, live stock, etc. This class of settlement will in the end sustain a larger population than the southerly parts served by the Canadian Pacific. The outstanding problem of the National railways in the West is unquestionably rapid colonization, with a view to the creation of the largest possible volume of profitable traffic.

As to the Eastern section of the National system, it is obvious, that the "clay belt" lands along the National Transcontinental in Western Ontario present a special problem in colonization that might well engage special attention. This is essentially a proposition that lends itself most effectively to colony settlement on the part of a class of people willing to go into a country remote from civilization and to take up the task of clearing land. That class can be found neither in Great Britain nor in the United States. Efforts towards colonizing French-Canadians could profitably be made. They have always had a preference for wooded areas. The only possible hope, however, of settling that country systematically and expeditiously, lies in bringing colonists direct from Europe, through a special agency organization. Suitable inducements must also be offered to these settlers by the State, particularly an adjustment of freight rates to ensure a profitable market for pulpwood for the pioneer period. The Scandinavian countries, particularly Norway and Sweden, as well as Finland, should offer the best field for specialized effort in this direction.

◆

This is the "morning after." We are well over our railway "spree." We are just wakening up to the sickening realization that we must now proceed to pay the price for incompetent administration and political debauchery. The wild spectacle of the past twenty years of railway construction seems like a dream; no attempt at co-ordination or system; branch lines, paralleling existing lines, freely chartered and guaranteed. The ambition of every western hamlet to have two or three systems competing for its trifling business has been gratified. No thought was given to the economic waste and the killing rates to which all this would ultimately lead.

Canada has, by passing enabling legislation and extending Government guarantees, wilfully and deliberately, brought into being the existing state of affairs. We must now shoulder the burden with the best possible grace we can, and proceed to live with our mile of railway for every 205 inhabitants, while the republic to the south, many times more highly developed, worries along with a mile for every 254 inhabitants. We have failed to realize that efficient transportation service and low rates are only the result of wise investment and good management. We elected the men who led us into all this, so it is only retributive justice that we should be called upon to pay the price of our own folly.

Our transportation situation today is in a mess—a most unholy mess. The most important factor in the development of a new country has been bungled in every conceivable manner and the problem of the Government now is to "unscramble" the eggs. We have been pushed headlong into the ownership and operation of what is now one of the greatest transportation systems of the world.

◆

Most of us in Canada have by this time lost our party orientation. We may still have "leanings," but the present political hodge-podge leaves one confused. New parties and policies will arise out of the ashes of discarded principles and party shibboleths. What worries me most is, whether, in the course of time, some opportunist political leader will arise and persuade his following that the cure for all Canada's transportation ills lies in the immediate absorption by the State of the Canadian Pacific system. Then, indeed, would our cup be full!

In a comprehensive and well-reasoned statement to the press, Mr. Beatty [president of the CPR] recently said:

. . . . The desire of everyone is that Canada should have to-day a railway system, or systems, so administered that the best service to the public will be obtained at the lowest rates consistent with fair wages, both for labour and capital. I say fair wages, because without them efficiency, loyalty and enterprise cannot be obtained, and without these things the quality of work which ensures efficient operation and low rates cannot be secured. The question therefore is: Will Government ownership bring about this result? The question sounds simple but is in reality complex. Theoretically much may be said in favour of Government ownership. Will those theories prove a failure initially, but correct themselves, in course of time, as their exponents may urge, how long a time can Canadian people afford to pay the losses on demoralized railroad service? Do they wish to launch out on the experiment now, or wait until their near neighbours, the United States, have worked out their experiment a little more satisfactorily? The cost of our own experiment could not fail to be great, a cost certain to be collected, directly or indirectly, from the pockets of the Canadian people. Railway men have an admirable slogan which I feel inclined to commend to the attention of the people of Canada at this moment, namely, "Stop, Look and Listen."

I have my own views on public ownership of railways, but they are not unalterable. I am undoubtedly prejudiced by an association with one company. That company has slowly developed to a point of efficiency and successful operation. Looking back over that history one is amazed at the importance of the part played by men whose enterprise, resourcefulness and tenacity of purpose could not, I think, have been stimulated and given rein in any Civil Service. It has taken more than thirty odd years to make the C.P.R. as efficient as it is to-day. It was not easy. The consciousness that it is so easily shattered is largely responsible for the constant and intense ambition on the part of officers and men to maintain, and even improve on, the tradition.

. . . We do not know enough that is encouraging about Government operation of large railway systems to justify any further excursions into that field at this time. To argue from the experience of old countries where civil service obtains a much better share of the ambitious young men than in Canada, or to argue from the alleged success of comparatively local affairs, or Government organizations dominated by exceptional personalities, is unfair—not to the railways, but to the country which has so much at stake in this issue. We can well afford to wait, to study dispassionately our own situation, and the experiment of the United States, before committing our country to serious changes in policy. . . .

◆

When we come to analyze the present railway problems in Canada and to seek the causes that led the country into the unpardonable and almost hopeless position we now find ourselves in, it will be clear that almost the chief responsibility lies at the doors of our Western provincial governments, who, purely for political purposes, and usually on the eve of general elections, undertook to guarantee the bonds of branch-line extensions so as to be able to go to the electorate on a "strong" railway policy. If such provincial guarantees had not been forthcoming, the Canadian Northern system, at least, could not have been financed. The Province of Manitoba had undertaken contingent liability in this respect to the extent of 25 million dollars, Saskatchewan 42 millions, Alberta 59 millions and British Columbia 81 million dollars! The Federal Government was then compelled to step in and take over the entire system, thus practically relieving the various provinces of a financial responsibility that might easily have brought them to the verge of bankruptcy.

Here lies another fatal weakness in our constitutional scheme—the principle of divided authority in the chartering of railways. We have seen that in the end the responsibility must fall on the Federal Government. We have now, or are about to have, two great railway systems in Canada. Neither of them will require inducements to provide adequate facilities anywhere in Canada. Each of them is perfectly able to finance extensions without guarantees. Such being the case, what justification exists for leaving in the hands of provincial authorities powers to charter new lines for political purposes, which might force the hands of the Government system or, at any rate, prove seriously embarrassing?

In the United States, they are now endeavouring to get away from the absurd spectacle of dual control of railway matters, under which State legislatures have the power to impose all sorts of ridiculous restrictions on the operation of railways within the State boundaries. This has been a fruitful source of annoyance and loss and has been largely responsible for the low physical condition some of the roads found themselves in when the war broke out. We should follow suit in Canada and vest in the Federal authorities complete control and sole jurisdiction with respect to railways, and to their chartering and capitalization.

SEVEN

The Labourer and His Hire

IN THESE DAYS THE subject of industrial relations is the favourite
theme of conversation where men foregather. Limited or complete
Government control of great industries and transportation during
the war, and Government jurisdiction over wages and industrial
earnings, which automatically followed, seem to have created a
new precedent, which appeals irresistibly to the imagination of the
worker. He now thinks he sees the end of "capitalism" and the
dawn of a new era. There is consequently much irresponsible talking, chiefly on the part of the professional labour agitator, who pre-
fers that sort of occupation even to a six-hour day of honest work.

Ominous statements are made from time to time indicating serious unrest on the part of labour. Mr. Tom Moore, President of the
Trades and Labour Congress of Canada, at a Canadian Club lun-
cheon in Toronto, recently said, in part:

> ... I tell you, if you are content to wait until revolution has
> taken place, you will have the upheaval in Canada as they had it
> in Russia...
>
> I know the temper of labour, and I know that it is one that in-
> sists that it shall reap a fuller reward for its share in industry. I
> am not afraid of unrest, I rather welcome unrest. But we want to
> see unrest of a practical nature, such as diverted into channels of
> construction. We must construct unrest in such a way that it will

bring the greatest amount of happiness. But unfortunately today, not all unrest is being diverted into channels of construction. . . .

Happiness shall be the measure of efficiency for the future. . . .

What steps can be taken to this end? The first need is to relieve the worker of some of his toil. It is the worker who should profit by the improvements of machinery and modern industry. . . .

Labour in Canada has seldom enjoyed outstanding leadership. The Gompers type has been conspicuous by its absence and no leader has apparently enjoyed the confidence of organized labour for more than a brief period. Mr. Moore seems, however, to be a broad-gauge individual and not afraid to speak his mind to his constituents. Trade unionism in Canada has been destructive more often than constructive. What substantial advantages labour has gained in the past have not been won by constitutional means, but rather by the cruder method of industrial warfare. This is a sad commentary.

The life of the labour leader is not a happy one. He is made the target of torrents of abuse by the rank and file of his own class. He obviously cannot "lead" and also hold a regular job at union wages. But as soon as he becomes the salaried employee of the organization, he automatically loses caste with his fellows. If he is one of the high officers of a central labour body, he is, in the discharge of his duties, called upon to meet prominent men in business and public life. It is becoming the fashion now to consult labour. However extreme he may have been in his views, he soon finds that employers are generally very approachable and quite decent fellows, earnestly anxious to assist in improving the lot of their employees. After a while the labour leader broadens out and becomes more tolerant. He is then apt to be accused of having betrayed the "cause" and sold out to capital. Labour has a lesson to learn. Leaders must be selected not out of admiration for the particular brand of fiery oratory they are able to deliver, but rather for their integrity and common sense. And they must be loyally supported and not made targets of venomous attacks by jealous competitors for office. Labour must practise loyalty to leaders, and team work.

———————◆———————

Now let us get down to a consideration of fundamentals. Our whole civilization is built on a basis of reward for services. This reward, usually paid in money, the individual utilizes to buy his meals, his bed, his clothes, etc. Certain men work very hard and spend very little and, in the course of years, accumulate a surplus. That is "capital." If put in a savings bank, this capital earns a reward for the owner. That is "interest." The bank in turn lends this "capital" to a manufacturer, who uses it, in his business, and pays the bank a reward for the privilege out of the profitable utilization of such loan. This is what we call "capitalism." If, however, the bank lent this money to the Government, who utilized it in building or operating a shoe factory, the Government must still pay interest for the privilege and, therefore, exact a profit on each pair of shoes made. But then we should call it socialism! How can "capitalism" or the "profit system" be abolished without utterly destroying our civilization and reverting to barbarism? We are merely confounding terms.

We find then, that neither Governments, individuals nor corporations can get the use of capital without compensation. Also that capital must ordinarily be profitably employed to pay this compensation. You can call this profit on capital "dividend," or you can call it "interest." It comes to precisely the same thing. As long as we have currency or, in fact, any convenient medium of exchange, we shall have savings, i.e., capital. We shall also have a lending and a borrowing class, as the world has had from time immemorial. We obviously cannot abolish the use of borrowed capital or the profit system, i.e., capitalism, without also abolishing the official medium of exchange as well as all individual property rights. That at once clears the atmosphere.

The inquiry that now faces us within each industry is (1) What is a fair reward for labour? (2) What is a fair reward for capital? I take it that these points are entirely legitimate subjects for investigation and discussion and contain in a nut-shell all the worker is really vitally interested in. His problem is not to invent some silly new social system, but to see that he gets his proper fair reward now. Capital must come down from its high horse. Liberty to capital is conceded; license is not. Inordinate profit persisted in will bring self-destruction in its train. Labour has its claims and the consumer will have something to say to the profiteer as well. The war may be over, but the "new spirit" remains. We must have a fair deal all round, and woe be unto him who blocks the way!

———————◆———————

The war has brought to the surface many uncomfortable questions for our statesmen to ponder over. The most uncomfortable of all is doubtless, the whole problem of the relations of capital to labour.

Our greatest need today is stability in industrial relations. How can this be even hoped for with local unions of every trade represented in every town between the Atlantic and the Pacific, each separate unit fighting its own local battles in its own clumsy, ruthless way? Labour under such conditions also becomes itinerant, naturally gravitating to the centres enjoying the highest union scale. Is there any necessity or justification for this preposterous continuous turmoil? Is there any valid reason today for variation in wage scale within most trades? The cost-of-living statistics clearly show that there is little or no difference in living expenses anywhere in Canada now. If, however, there is any necessity at all for differentiation, it surely could be amply provided for by an Eastern and Western minimum scale based on official cost-of-living figures.

Employers throughout Canada would also be in a much better position under uniform and more stable wage conditions. Competition would be on a fairer basis and contracts could be entered into for longer periods with the assurance that irresponsible agitators could not precipitate strikes in advance of the termination of existing agreements. Labour would also feel that Dominion-wide investigations and agreements dealing with wages and working conditions in each trade would be more likely to be based on justice and fairness to the worker, than the purely local victories that may be gained.

It is however obvious that a uniform wage scale could not blindly be imposed in connection with all trades. Underground mining earnings, for instance, being almost invariably on a contract basis, are essentially governed by local physical mining conditions. Cost-of-living also is not, by any means, the infallible test or the sole factor to be considered. Climatic conditions might seriously limit the number of possible working days in the year in any particular district. Seasonal occupations also might require special consideration. The new spirit will concede to labour the right to proper cognizance of enforced idle time and its effect on annual earnings. It is not the daily but the annual income that must in the end govern.

We cannot set back the hands of the clock at will. Labour unrest is not a product of today or yesterday—it has been with us in increasing volume for many years. Its present solution is going to be the job of a real statesman, far-seeing, wise and sympathetic. Whatever the final outcome, the verdict of the next generation will be that the predatory, autocratic and altogether stupid employer, whether he falls within the capitalist class or not, must shoulder the blame, as well as the consequences, just as the blame for our present drastic prohibition measures falls justly on the shoulders of the rapacious, unprincipled class which made the barroom the sink of iniquity and immorality that finally destroyed it and all its works.

In the meanwhile, we have been blundering along in Canada without any attempt being made to create machinery to set our industrial house in order. We have machinery to deal with industrial disputes, but none to prevent them! The situation is growing more desperate each day and the breach between labour and capital is widening. The Western Labour Federation in a recent convention frankly declared war on capital. The only official remedy so far offered is to increase our military establishment!

◆

The Industrial Reconstruction Council in Great Britain is a body having for its object propaganda with a view to awakening a national interest in the need for a complete system of industrial autonomy. This council strongly favours the "Whitley scheme," which has now been adopted by the British War Cabinet as part of its reconstruction policy.

The central idea in the Whitley scheme is absolutely and admittedly sound, which is more than can be said for Canada's present labour legislation, designed solely to cure the evil when prevention is what modern society demands.

The underlying principle of this plan is a realization that each industry is a unit with its own problems to solve. The scheme contemplates the organization of an "Industrial Council" within each industry, possibly embracing collateral industries as well. The idea is to bring together, for the solution of questions of mutual interest, all the factors in each trade, representing capital, management and labour.

There is not to be the slightest interference with the Trade Union organization. As a matter of fact, the hope is entertained that the Trade Union should be, if anything, more of a factor than it has been in the past. Nor is it the intention that there should be any interference with the individual management of industries. An industrial council would be composed of representatives of associations of employers and associations of working people and would thus become a Parliament, or representative body, for the discussion of all matters referred to it by employers, men, or management, and by any legislative enactment. No Council can be formed without the consent of both employers and employed.

Mr. Whitley himself summarizes the main objects of the plan in the following language:

> ... We want to destroy suspicion between employer and workers and put in its place a mutual confidence born of mutual understanding. We seek to regularize employment, impart industrial training, utilize inventions, prosecute industrial research, improve design and quality and promote legislation affecting workshop conditions.
>
> Hitherto the employers have had rather too much to say in industry. Our organization is triple in character—in workshops, in

districts and nationality. Thus we feel that we can come to grips with a problem in all its enormous detail—works, rules, distribution, working hours, peace prices, methods of wage payments, grievances, holidays, physical welfare, discipline, terms of engagement, training apprentices, technical libraries, suggestions for improvement in methods, investigations of the causes of reduced efficiency, collections for clubs and charities, entertainment and sport. . . .

The most important feature of the scheme is to furnish a body where labour problems can be deliberated upon and solved. It is not the intention that the industrial councils should take the place of wages-boards, but it is expected that the question of contract between employer and employee could be most effectively dealt with by a body of this sort in each separate trade and with some degree of certainty that the sacredness of contract would be respected by both parties.

It will perhaps look somewhat drastic even to suggest the idea of a maximum reward for the use of industrial capital. The principle involved, however, cannot be successfully assailed. In order to ensure that even-handed justice shall be meted out to all, the modern State now absolutely controls railway capitalisation and rates. How long would the country tolerate extravagant dividends on railway capital without demanding rate revision? There is apparently no particular reason why capital employed in any other enterprise should be regarded as more sacred and inviolate than railways capital and be given *carte blanche* to exploit its labour, or prey on the consumer.

◆

But apart entirely from any future State restrictions upon returns on industrial capital, the present tendency is very distinctly towards the elimination of spectacular profits. Labour is becoming increasingly insistent upon the most favourable terms for itself and concessions will doubtless be forced in each industry until capital, with all the cards laid on the table, is able to convince the worker that the absolute limit of safety has been reached. In the end, outside competition will, of course, absolutely determine the limit of reward to capital as well as to labour.

But, while the proposal to admit labour representation to participate in the actual business management of industry is theoretically sound, it is open to certain very material objections. Labour has apparently no definite policy on the subject beyond the hackneyed assertion that the worker, being equally as important as capital in our industrial scheme, is, therefore, entitled to equal participation in the dictation of business policy. This is a false conclusion based on very defective reasoning.

The lack of understanding and indecision shown by organised labour in its relations with capital are almost pathetic. There are leaders of every shade of opinion on the subject, ranging all the way from ultra Conservatives to those who preach Bolshevik doctrine and even go beyond. The mind of the rank and file is confounded with high sounding, but meaningless, phrases, such as the "democratisation of industry" and the "abolition of capitalism." These, of course, lend themselves readily to oratorical flights. What does it all mean? Do we want to go even farther than the Russian lunatics who, by the way, have not even commenced to abolish capitalism? They have stolen the savings of millions of, more or less, deserving people and have appropriated the same for the benefit of the State. They have also filched the savings of still more deserving people in other countries by repudiating their external debt and seizing property representing foreign investment. Meanwhile they are printing spurious "money" by the billion. Why? Because the State can no longer borrow. No one will trust it. So it manufactures its own money. That is, it issues formal "promises to pay" and that, of course, is capitalism. The time will come when a workman, earning perhaps a thousand roubles per month, will not be able to buy his three meals a day with it, just because his money is worthless. There is neither value nor security behind it.

We have in Canada an external capital liability of at least five billion dollars. We also have an additional internal investment of some thirteen billions. All this money is employed in our railways, industries, mines, farms, etc. We do not owe this vast amount to either Rockefeller or to Morgan. It chiefly represents the accumulated savings, through weary years, of millions of hard working, frugal people, in Canada and in foreign countries, some now living and some dead. A multitude of orphans, widows, aged, infirm and humble people the world over, depend upon the returns from this investment for their daily bread. Insurance funds, trust funds—savings of all sorts—make up the bulk of this huge investment. An inconsiderable part of it is, of course, owned by "bloated" capitalists, but we cannot discriminate, except through the channel of income taxation, which we are already doing. Is anyone sufficiently crazy or unmoral to suggest seriously that Canada should formally steal this money by confiscating property and abolishing all right of private possession? That is just what they did in Russia.

Until labour assumes financial responsibility, as an investor, or contributor guaranteed in some way, it obviously cannot share in the dictation of business policy. Incidentally, one of the chief obstacles to successful Government operation of industry, is precisely this very absence of financial responsibility on the part of a paid management, with nothing to lose in case of failure beyond a job. The position of the labourer director or executive would be identically the same.

Labour's relationship to industrial management is not, however, the only question to be considered. It is generally admitted that capital has been selfish and predatory in its attitude towards the worker. But labour presently organised and became reasonably successful in obtaining redress of its grievances. The consumer, on the other hand, has been absolutely helpless. He also feels that he has been exploited. To be quite frank, it is doubtful whether existing industrial relationship is nearly as important an issue, from the point of view of the welfare of the general public, as the joint attitude of capital and labour towards the patient consumer. Strikes, resulting in higher pay for transportation workers, for instance, forthwith give birth to correspondingly increased rates on railways and street car systems. Increased wages for miners are followed by increased coal prices. The load is instantly transferred to the public, which was probably not represented in the settlement of the dispute at all.

Past experience and past record give the consumer no assurance whatever that labour controlling industry would be less unscrupulous and less predatory than capital has been.

———————◆———————

Many of those who loudly deplore the present condition of labour, and sympathetically refer to the worker as a "wage slave," are equally emphatic in their denunciation of the "profit system." The inference is, I presume, that industry should not be carried on for profit or gain. Does that vague and peculiar creed mean that no interest is to be paid on capital invested in industry? Or does it mean that labour, having control, may freely take any profits it chooses by way of extravagant wages? Or is the State to conscript labour to manufacture at cost for the benefit of the consumer, paying for such services in food, lodging, clothes and medical attendance? Or does all this sensational vapouring merely indicate that we are, at present, economically out of balance and that the reward paid to capital, the wages paid to labour and the price paid by the consumer should be readjusted? There is, apparently only one way to abolish the "profit system" and that is to abolish individual property rights, and our monetary system and then to put everyone to work for the State, which would pay for his keep. This is advanced socialism.

Let us try to visualise the modern Utopia functioning on such a plan. Imagine that the following simple story is from the "Official Eye Witness." We may, one of these days, read its exact counterpart in the Russian newspapers. . . . Individual ownership of property had been abolished, which necessarily also involved the abolition of wages. We proudly ceased to be Wages Slaves. Under the new dispensation we were all working for a meal ticket. If, by the way, we lost it, we simply had to file an application in triplicate for a new one and cheerfully starve until we received it. Of course, we could not borrow. We were entitled to one pair of trousers annually (regulation pattern), and if we wore the knees out prematurely, we were sternly commanded to parade before a Board of Inquiry to show cause why we should not be incarcerated for the reckless use of Government property. Our trousers were indubitably public property. Of course, no one ever surreptitiously appropriated our borrowed belongings, because all men had become simple, honest and industrious by Act of Parliament.

The pre-digested, standard meal, compounded by Government, was a veritable poem. Back in the dark, unenlightened pre-socialistic days, when every individual minded his own business with a minimum of State assistance, opinions used to differ as to what we should eat and what we should drink—particularly as to the latter. But a new era happily dawned. The dyspeptic now devoured with impunity his ration of the Standard bully beef stew, regardless of consequences, resting secure in the potency of the famous Act of Parliament standardising the human stomach. The Hebrew recklessly consumed his ham and the Roman Catholic his Friday roast beef, religion and the Creator having been abolished for failure to conform to the official standard pattern. The socialistic State obviously could not consistently recognise any Superior Being. The use of tobacco, Government Brand, became compulsory, with occasional disastrous consequences. The socialised State ever meted out impartial justice!

Our educational system at first proved a troublesome issue. Later it was absolutely standardised. It goes without saying that the State could not tolerate special privileges or opportunities being accorded anyone, such a policy would inevitably have led to undemocratic intellectual inequality. To entirely overcome the danger of this, a simple Act of Parliament was quietly slipped through making the stupid wise over night, and reducing those endowed with exceptional wisdom and intelligence to the official intellectual standard. Competition and ambition were necessarily completely abolished. No worthy patriotic citizen would even wish to rise above the dead level. Besides, why worry? Were we not all working for the irreducible minimum of three meals per day and a standard Government bed with the loan of the necessary clothing? We were all kings!

Candidly, we nearly came to blows on the question of occupations. This problem we soon found contained the crux of the whole situation. In the socialistic State—founded on the theory of absolutely equality—self-determination or individual choice of occupation could not, of course, for a moment be countenanced. Neither could the merit system. Promotion became obsolete and also, of course, discipline. The State officially declared all occupations equally important and honourable and desirable. We however, experienced some difficulty in persuading the men in the stoke-hole that they were just as pleasantly situated as the captain of the ship, but eventually they recognised the truth and smothered their unworthy ambition. Everyone worked his silly head off solely from a sense of public duty. At first, some men actually preferred a medical career to that of an undertaker, while aspiring and hopeful embryo bank-managers foolishly expressed disappointment at being assigned to honourable janitorships. But the nation's work had to be done. Some quite unique innovations were incorporated in the new occupational scheme. The streets, of course, had to be swept, rags picked and old bottles collected. These, being light jobs, suitable for the aged, ultimately furnished an excellent and congenial retiring opportunity for cabinet ministers, college professors and railway and bank presidents. The white overalls and the push cart became an outward and visible sign of nobility—a reward gracefully conferred upon distinguished citizens at the close of a more strenuous career in the public service.

But dark days eventually overtook this ideal democracy. The people began to mutter. It was being dimly realised that the modern overseer was just a stupid, arrogant official. He became an object of intense hatred. We even lamented the exit of the defunct capitalist employer of the old regime. Instead of being "wage slaves" we had merely become slaves without wages! Finally, an inspired reformer wrote a new and up-to-date version of "Uncle Tom's Cabin"—and Utopia was triumphantly emancipated.

◆

A plea for a broad spirit of toleration is in order. The employer falls mentally into the error of associating the employee with the proverbial highwayman with the motto: "Stand and deliver." Labour, on the other hand, is apt to picture the employer with horns on and cloven feet; as an unfeeling slave driver, rolling in luxury, whose sole object in life is to amass wealth at the expense of his "wage slaves," as the demagogue is fond of calling the employee. One has only to enter a motion picture theatre, almost at random, to find this conception of the case vividly thrown on the screen in a lurid melodrama and with all the harrowing detail. This view is evidently popular among the masses. Incidentally, if the motion picture censors would give less attention to the accidental display of a bare leg or a wine bottle, and more to this pernicious propaganda to poison further the relations between employer and employee, they might perform valuable public services.

The Great War has had the effect of putting the socialist to the fire test and, incidentally, has brought home to many workers some very unpleasant truths in regard to this much advertized, but little understood, system. No one can tell just what the socialist platform is. It is "all things to all men." Stripped of all camouflage, we might call it "humanitarianism." It is the creed that everyone is entitled to work. That the remuneration shall be fair and the hours shall be reasonably limited. It is the same creed as that taught by Our Saviour and subscribed to by every decent civilized man since the world has enjoyed civilization.

The great majority of employers in Canada have been on both sides of the question. The private life of the employer is of course, generally surrounded with more comforts than that of the employee. This gives rise to envy and jealousy. It is, however, a rash assumption to maintain that he gets more out of life than those of his employees who receive sufficient wages to dress, eat and sleep under decent conditions, and few of them do not. The employer generally works longer hours, sleeps fewer hours and eats less. The burden of responsibility rests on his shoulders. Few industrial concerns escape being confronted with grave crises from time to time, which drain the very life blood of those who have to face and solve them. The average small industry in Canada, which is the backbone of our industrial life, gives little more than a living for those engaged in it. The spectacular earnings are made in the large, merged industries that are able to eliminate competition and control markets. The path of industrial progress in Canada is literally strewn with failures, and the man who ultimately brings an industry into the safe haven of success has probably given the country more than he himself ever received.

Years ago, I dreamed dreams, as an unsophisticated young man should. I saw myself as a captain of industry—a sort of benevolent Ironmaster. That was immediately after I had been forced to acquire, through a chain of circumstances, a controlling interest in two western manufacturing concerns. I devoted myself, heart and soul to my task, but could not spare time to take the actual management into my own hands. For long periods the directors literally sweated blood over the problems that confronted them, and, incidentally, I devoted much capital that I could ill spare from other interests, to the development of these industries. To-day my actual cash investment, over a period of fourteen years, is no trifling amount. It has, however, been most illuminating experience, which I do not in the least regret.

I have just received the last annual statement of the larger of these industries. We manufactured $116,000 worth of goods. Our labour outlay was little over $58,000, raw materials $37,000, overhead $18,000 and estimate profits $3,000. None of the shareholders, I should add, ever received a dollar's worth of dividend or salary or any benefit whatsoever from this investment. We have, on the contrary, voluntarily cancelled over fifty thousand dollars of common stock and bonds paid for in full, to take up losses on operation. I have spent many sleepless nights over it all. Our plant is modern and in excellent condition. We have never had labour trouble, because every just grievance has always been corrected. Most of the employees are highly skilled men and have been with us for years, and are my very good personal friends. We have, at least, three different unions to deal with. Two of our employees act on our Board of Directors and on the Executive Committee. Our management has varied, but is now faultless and the industry is one needed in its community. But whenever we get to the point where a reasonable profit is in sight, we are invariably face to face with an increased cost for labour! We have now, I believe, at last turned the corner. But it has taken many weary years. This is the literal truth. I often ask myself, pointedly: "Where do I come in?"

I do not wish, in submitting this little human document, to attempt to mislead. Such an experience as mine is not, of course, universal, but it is by no means uncommon. The development of a successful industry is frequently a slow and heart-breaking process. The chief owner of the smaller industry when he personally undertakes the management, which he generally does, gets little more return for the use of his capital, experience and services, than a very moderate income. Labour is very apt to base all arguments on the earnings of the spectacular, monopolistic industries. That is no criterion at all. The backbone of our industrial structure is the smaller industries of the country.

◆

Soon after Mr. Gompers' famous ultimatum to employers south of the line, one of their great weeklies, "The Saturday Evening Post," in commenting on his attitude, summed the matter up very fairly and completely as follows:

> It was not necessary for Mr. Gompers to serve notice that union labour will oppose any attempt to reduce wages. That is a matter of course. But the union-wage scale tells only half the story as to the condition of labour. The other half is told by the degree of employment or unemployment. A high union-wage scale does no good if labour is not at work.
>
> Labour is the largest item in the cost of goods. The American wage scale is much higher than any in Europe. If American labour is to be fully employed, or even relatively so, American goods must find a market abroad in competition with European goods. Nobody but a hopeless blockhead wants lower wages for their own sake. Nobody wants unemployment. The practical question is: How can we pay decidedly more for labour and still sell goods in free, competitive markets? For unless we do sell goods in such markets we shall finally have idle labour.

There is only one possible answer: Our labour must be more efficient than the labour with which its products compete.

It can be more efficient through its own superior skill and diligence, through using better tools—that is, better machinery—through superior, industrial organization and leadership.

Every obstacle to the most effective organization and leadership sets the pointer to lower wages. Every handicap on invention, on ability, on improvement throughout the process of production and distribution menaces the wage scale. Every burden upon production through avoidable capital-and-labour rows is inimical to it. I.W.W., with its sabotage and general hostility to production, spells peril for it. Labour that proposes not only to get the highest possible wage, but to give the smallest possible return in productive effort is a drag on the wage scale.

Nobody's sentiments are going to cut any particular figure in the answer. We can pay decidedly more for a day's work than Europe pays and still sell the product of our day's work as cheap as Europe can—or cheaper. But the only possible way of doing it is to produce more or better goods in a day. We cannot pay decidedly more for labour than our competitors pay, unless our labour on the whole is decidedly more efficient. Every handicap to the most efficient application of American labour lessens its chance of maintaining this wage scale with full employment.

The logic of the foregoing is irrefutable.

———————◆———————

In considering the question of a fair division of profits upon industry as between capital and labour, the investigator finds himself confronted with a great deal of shallow thinking. Unfortunately, there are vast difficulties in the way of obtaining reliable statistics on this subject.

The Dominion Census Bureau has, however, compiled some illuminating figures bearing on Canada's industrial production. These figures do not pretend to be absolutely complete and correct, but they cover 35,000 industries, which is quite sufficiently extensive for all practical purposes. In a bulletin recently issued, further detail is given, which, with judicious estimating, is almost sufficiently complete to enable one to construct Profit and Loss Statement covering the operation of Canadian industries for the year 1917, which apparently cannot be very far wrong.

The total output is given as $3,015,506,869. The average wage of the worker was apparently $738 and the net profit of industry $592 on each wage earner's effort during the year. The following items enter into the cost of production:

Sales		$3,015,506,869
Salaries	$95,983,506	
Wages	457,245,456	
Materials	1,602,820,631	
General Overhead	239,373,046	
Depreciation Reserve	150,000,000	
Bad Debt Reserve	30,000,000	
Fuel	73,087,840	
Estimated Profit	366,996,390	
	$3,015,506,869	$3,015,506,869

Deducting the cost of production, $2,648,510,479, from the value of the total output gives us $366,996,390 as the estimated net profit, which represents about 13¼ per cent profit on the total investment of 2,773 million dollars. But it is safe to estimate that at least one-third of the total investment represents bond and other preferred capital on an average interest basis that would not exceed 6 per cent. We must also make due allowance for the fact that the remaining two-thirds of the alleged capital is unquestionably inflated. To what extent it would be difficult to estimate, but, I think, we could safely reduce the total invested common stock capital, from two-thirds of the total to not more than one-half. This would give us, roughly, one billion of capital, earning a fixed rate of interest of 6 per cent, or 60 million dollars. Deducting this from the total earnings gives us approximately 300 millions to apply as earnings on the actual common stock investment of about 1,500 millions, which would be a 20 per cent basis.

A return of 13¼ per cent cannot be considered extravagant on industrial investment in view of the risks involved and also taking into consideration the fact that 1917 was a war year with somewhat greater returns on capital than under normal conditions. The gist of the matter probably is that the average small competitive industry in Canada made during 1917 a very fair return on capital. The larger, highly protected and monopolistic enterprises, in all likelihood made the spectacular earnings. It is also fair to assume that a ten year average, under normal conditions, would almost certainly show a basis of net earnings well below that of 1917.

So we finally arrive at the conclusion that, speaking generally, there is not very much to spare from the present estimated normal net earnings on industrial capital in Canada to permit of any important general increase in wages. Nor can the worker apparently look to any considerable extent to schemes of profit-sharing to increase his earnings materially. From whatever angle we regard the matter, we find ourselves confronted with the uncomfortable situation that, if higher wages are to be paid to Canadian industrial workers, it is quite evident that no considerable part of the burden can be assumed by capital. The bulk of the load must be transferred to the ultimate consumer, by means of higher prices for industrial products, resulting in a still higher cost of living all around: this will, of course, further curtail the purchasing power of the worker's dollar. The load however must be so transferred, if such transfer is possible. Other countries may produce more cheaply and undersell Canadian industries in the domestic market. Then there will be pressure brought to bear for increased protective duties, or—our industries will become bankrupt and the worker lose his job. There seems no other alternative.

I am not trying to make a case for capitalism or to construct an apology for our present system of industrial management. My object merely is to endeavour to place the situation judicially and impartially before the worker and before capital. There is no useful object served in shutting one's eyes to obvious facts. We are unquestionably confronted with a crisis in our industrial relations. It is perhaps largely fostered by an erroneous conception of the actual situation, for there was never a time in the history of our country when clear thinking and plain speaking were such a necessity as they are today.

◆

The minimum wage agitation is worthy of deep consideration. It is nothing new. In the Fifteenth Century, magistrates in England, under Act of Parliament, fixed standard wages for agricultural labour. Certainly, the right of labour to a decent minimum wage cannot be challenged. If an industry is unable to pay a fair wage, based on cost of living, it had better perish. It is, of course, absolutely futile to accept cases like the Ford Company as a fair comparison. While this concern is able to pay a minimum wage of $6.00 per day to its employees, it is to be noted carefully that, at the same time, it can distribute 200 per cent profits to its shareholders! There are few other industries in Canada in such a favourable position, perhaps none. It is quite in a class by itself.

Whatever may be the attitude of the State towards the principle of a living minimum wage for labour generally, however, there is one aspect of the case that cannot safely be ignored in a civilized country, namely, the moral duty that rests on the community to ensure that a decent minimum is fixed at least in the case of female labour. That becomes a social question primarily. Much progress has been made in this direction by large industrial concerns in the United States. One of them, employing an enormous number of women, has recently decided upon a minimum of $16.50 per week. Conditions in our larger Canadian cities in this respect are shocking. The Federal Government until recently employed girls in Ottawa at salaries below $10 a week!

◆

It is possible that the hours of labour are too long in many occupations. The plan of introducing a six-hour day is now being tried. A large commercial concern in Toronto is also going to experiment on a five-day week, which seems sound for a commercial business, if generally enforced. There is room for much constructive work and earnest investigation here. We rail at the miner for not working his full six days a week. But how many of us understand that working thousands of feet underground with artificial light, under trying atmospheric conditions and surrounded by the dangers prevailing in many mines, tries the nerves of these men sorely, almost beyond human endurance. Steady work day after day becomes impossible.

I cannot, however, agree that 44 hours work per week is beyond what might reasonably be expected from the average human being, in most occupations. Some occupations, I grant, take more out of the human frame than others and should receive special consideration. But a general standard is dangerous. We are bound to increase production in Canada today to pay our war liabilities, and it surely cannot be done by further shortening the hours of labour. There is a school of benevolent theorists which maintains that shorter hours means greater efficiency. To a certain extent that is true. A man can possibly do as much in ten hours as he would do in twelve, but there is a limit somewhere. No sane person would expect the same result in production from four hours' work as from twelve. The old rule of eight hours' work, eight hours' play and eight hours' sleep is perhaps the happy medium.

Our population is growing slowly and laboriously. We have, as a rule, no unemployment problem, except perhaps during brief seasons. On the other hand, we have an almost perpetual labour scarcity. We cannot, therefore, shorten hours radically without decreasing production, which, with our present national liability, would be almost fatal. During short periods of extensive unemployment such might safely be done, but as an industrial policy it would be suicidal. In the seasonal occupations, such as the building trades, the workers have long enforced holidays during the winter. To shorten their hours further during the limited season in Canada is not sound.

There is another very important feature to be considered. In this age of strenuous industrial competition, when overhead expenses must be distributed over the largest possible output, it is evident

that capital investment in machinery, plant and equipment cannot
be permitted to lie idle for eighteen hours out of the twenty-four,
simply in order that labour may enjoy a six-hour day. The ability of
industry to pay fair wages depends solely on output. If labour
finally wins the six-hour day, it will be found that it will involve a
double   shift   in   most   industries,   the   first   shift   working
uninterruptedly from 7 a.m. to 1 p.m. and the second shift taking
on the work at the latter hour until 7 p.m. A single management
could handle an industry organized on such a basis, but until we
have a sufficient number of skilled men available to provide a
double shift for most Canadian industries it is obviously premature
to discuss seriously the six-hour day. On the basis indicated, most
industries could possibly run very economically and efficiently and
with a minimum of overhead expense in proportion to output, and
thus pay an increased wage per hour.

———————◆———————

I do not wish to write platitudes. But I find it hard to refrain from
having a tilt at the venerable fake notion, which seems to pervade
all classes, that labour is a necessary evil, an unpleasant duty, and
happy is he who neither works nor spins. Listen to this: "...
Labour is at once a burden, a chastisement, an honour and a
pleasure.... What were man, what were life, what were civilization, without labour? All that is great in man comes of labour—
greatness in art, in literature, in science. Knowledge—'The wing
wherewith we fly to heaven'—is only acquired through labour.
Genius is but a capability of labouring intensely: it is the power of
making great and sustained efforts. Labour may be a chastisement,
but it is indeed a glorious one. It is worship, duty, praise, and
immortality—for those who labour with the highest aims and for
the purest purposes...."

I worked hard all my life long, until, after a severe illness, I decided to retire from active effort, which I did for nearly two years.
This period proved the most drab, uninteresting and altogether un-
desirable in my career. I had plenty of resources within myself. I
was fond of reading, gardening, etc., and my days were fully oc-

cupied. But I could never get away from the idea that I was on the shelf—that my work was done. The absence of serious responsibility and of the wholesome influence of the regularity and self-discipline incidental to active business, reduced my life to the level of that of a mere animal. I would not repeat the experience under any consideration, so long as I am able to do a day's work.

A good friend of mine once said, in a discussion on what constituted happiness and satisfaction in life, that his conception of that illusive state was "a congenial and useful job well done." I feel that this represents the absolute truth. It does not matter a bit whether the particular job is the making of a pair of boots, writing a book, or winning an important case before the highest court in the land. The principle is precisely the same. Most of this talk about shorter hours and more holidays is founded on absolutely wrong premises. The inference is that any sort of useful occupation is a necessary evil and that happiness only lies in idleness, which is absolutely contrary to human experience. Our wage earners are imbibing this poisonous vapouring from professional agitators all over the country.

◆

The subject of factory control by labour is receiving much attention in Great Britain, where constructive thinking is the order of the day, just now. The State was forced into manufacturing during the war and owns many splendid plants. Sir Eric Geddes now proposes to turn over certain aviation plants to be operated by the workers on a co-operative basis and under a limited control by the State as owner.

Mr. H.G. Wells, as chairman of a committee appointed by the British Government to consider questions of labour in the aviation industry, recently made a minority report to the Committee on Civil Aerial Transport, embodying this suggestion. He recommended joint control of aircraft factories and aerial transport by the State and the workers. He also emphasized the value of this new industry in affording employment for disabled sailors and soldiers.

It is possible that a national aircraft factory at Waddon, where thousands of workers have been employed in the manufacture of powerful new aeroplanes, suitable for commercial purposes, may be selected as one of the factories where the experiment in democratized industry will be carried out. The following is an outline of a plan elaborated by the "shop stewards" at Waddon, for the working out of the proposal:

1. The factories are to be controlled on the business side by a committee representing jointly and equally the State as owner, and the workers as producers.
2. On the productive side the work should be controlled by a body representing the men and women in each department.
3. Under the committee should be the departmental heads constitutionally chosen by this committee, due regard being paid to their qualifications.
4. Trade union rates and standards should be regarded as the minimum, and nothing should be done to weaken the conditions already obtained by organized labour.

This is all refreshing evidence of new ground being broken.

———————◆———————

The question of wage disputes reduces itself merely to one of administration of plain justice as between man and man. The problem does not look formidable, stripped of all extraneous matter. The most complicated disputes, frequently involving precisely the same principles, are settled daily by our courts of justice. Before the war, the world could not agree to settle international disputes as private individuals were compelled to settle their quarrels. But the war has made international arbitration not alone possible, but absolutely compulsory. It will ultimately have the same effect in regard to the lesser questions. The world is sated with war. We will have none of it, whether it be war within or without our national boundaries.

The most damnable indictment lies against Canadian labour leaders. Having recognized the problem, they have been satisfied with a policy of opportunism. Our public men have still less cause to be proud. Successive Ministers of Labour have timidly played with the problem of capital v. labour. Capital itself has pursued a stupid course. It would be difficult to point to any great political or economic problem that has been made the victim of more arbitrary methods, studied negligence and lack of vision, than this. We now have the problem before us in acute form. It cannot be side-stepped any longer. It seems to be a case of whether one side or the other has the bigger club, which is a thoroughly German method of settling grievances or attaining ambitions.

------------------------------ ◆ ------------------------------

Labour has always been most insistent upon its "right to strike."

Under democratic government, such as we have in Canada, and such as they have in the United States, where most international labour union organizations maintain their headquarters, a position of extreme danger is necessarily created, when any class of the community, be the members thereof mechanics, labourers, farmers or bankers, can hold a loaded gun at the head of the government and the people, at a critical time in the history of the country, and enforce any and all demands, be they just or unjust, simply by the threat to demoralize business, backed up by an enormous political power. Democratic government becomes a farce under such conditions.

The right to strike under any circumstances also confers the right to deprive citizens of transportation, fuel, bread and all the necessities of life, the right to let criminals loose on society, and to deprive the community of fire protection. Society has, as a matter of fact, during recent years been deprived of all these things from time to time in different parts of the world through strikes. Decidedly, this right cannot be conceded in a reorganized, civilized community. Some better way must be discovered.

The labour union movement has served its main purposes in securing better pay and shorter hours for employees in certain branches of industrial production. To bring about these excellent reforms, the unions organized for fighting purposes. It would be a grave error to condemn unstintingly a fighting organization. The unpleasant fact remains that few worth-while social readjustments have ever been attained solely through moral suasion. Self-interest lies at the bottom of all human endeavour, and privilege dies hard. We concede the point and make the sacrifice more often because we *have to,* than because we *want to,* and the "big stick" is generally the only conclusive argument. This situation reflects little credit on our state of society, but history is replete with instances that demonstrate the truth of the assertion. Labour assuredly would never have reached its present status without militant methods. They cannot therefore be unreservedly condemned. It was a case of the end justifying the means. But with the end of this world war the days of the fighting organization should become a thing of the past; it won't fit in with the New Spirit.

———————◆———————

Canada, with her pitiful eight and a half million inhabitants and with her large liability for pensions, public debt, etc., and vast expenditure for the ordinary services of Government, to some extent necessitated by the enormous area of country to be administered and served, is today precisely in the same position as a highly capitalized industrial establishment with commodious buildings, modern machinery and equipment, as well as organization and markets available for a large annual output and, naturally, burdened with all the overhead expenses incidental to such a manufacturing equipment and capacity, but with two-thirds of the plant standing idle owing to lack of labour. The problem confronting this imaginary enterprise and the present financial problem of the Dominion of Canada appear to be absolutely identical. It is contained in two main propositions: first, so to utilize the present available forces as to obtain maximum efficiency and the greatest possible output; secondly, to obtain at the earliest moment a sufficient number of additional hands to run the plant to capacity.

Our greatest national problem is doubtless to find the hands to work our agricultural lands, our mines, our fisheries and our forest resources, to capacity or as near capacity as we can. Granting the available resources and the available manpower, additional working capital will naturally follow as fast as required. If capital gets fair protection and profitable employment in Canada, we need concern ourselves little about this phase of our development. The world is now full of capital looking for safe and profitable investment, as far from Bolshevik activities as possible.

Half of Europe is bootless and lacks almost every article that has hitherto been considered indispensable. Canada and the United States have also been living on short rations and will require to replenish. Our railways are out at elbow, our ships have been destroyed, our productive machinery requires overhauling. Everything, in fact, indicates that there will be no lack of orders or employment as soon as we get safely over the present transition period.

During the war the slacker was asked why he was not in khaki. The able-bodied industrial slacker might now appropriately be asked: "Why are you not in overalls?" Employers might advantageously follow the good, sound war practice of turning adrift strong, single men who occupy situations that could be satisfactorily filled by women, physically-disabled soldiers or married men. There will soon be man-sized jobs waiting elsewhere for the able-bodied worker.

The question of man-power must always be paramount in a new, undeveloped country and Canada is no exception. It is perhaps the supreme problem today. Labour in Canada has, naturally, always been antagonistic to immigration. Public policies on the subject consequently, have had to be framed with a cautious eye to labour's general attitude. There is just now a strong tendency to erect unreasonable barriers against the inflow of population. While it is sound policy to close our gates to undesirables, we frankly cannot afford to be too particular. "Canada for Canadians" is a beautiful sentiment, but Eastern Canada, with its dwindling birth rate, cannot furnish population for colonizing its own idle lands, leave alone the enormous areas of the West. Canada must perforce increase her population so as to reduce the per capita public liability and we must secure assistance to develop our country and increase production to pay our debts. This seems the most elementary sort of proposition. There is no philanthropy about it. It is plain, unadulterated business.

There is another feature of immigration that organized labour must not overlook. Colonization via the "homestead route" is not at all a pleasant occupation—not nearly as pleasant as urban employment with a six-hour day and a minimum wage. Yet, this tiresome frontier job of work must be done by someone, if urban labour is to continue drawing even its minimum wage and not be reduced to the point where even six hours' work a day is unobtainable. This pioneer is the man who, in the last analysis, pays part of the wages. Skilled labour has not in the past manifested any alarming tendency to take up frontier homesteads. The fact is that the development of our "hinterland" would cease almost as soon as we put the bars up against alien immigration. That is about the only class that will be bothered with our present homesteads consisting mainly of cull lands, remote from transportation.

----◆----

We find in the bewildering paradox of life that evil influences are frequently productive of beneficial ends. The course of our social evolution is punctuated with horrors, and mankind has in all ages waded through rivers of blood to reach the shore of the land of promise. The world has just emerged from another blood bath, the most appalling of all. The crucifixion of mankind was endured with stoicism because great principles were at stake, principles great enough to justify millions upon millions of the world's lusty youths risking the great sacrifice and ready to pay it willingly. Some degenerate minds saw in this world-eruption merely the hands of the "capitalist." Those with a clearer perception of things saw the world in arms to vindicate the right of the common man to liberty and freedom of action. This was gained at the cost of life and treasure, willingly sacrificed by all classes, in volume unprecedented in history.

The world is exhausted by the effort and the time is ripe for the unscrupulous demagogue to take advantage of the situation. Countries now at peace with other nations are seething with poisonous propaganda within, directed by those who stayed at home and profited by the nation's distress. Labour is restless and impatient and easily influenced. Strikes are the order of the day. Labour feels its power. Organizations no longer respect contracts, nor are they amenable to discipline. Society cannot resist organized anarchy on the part of a large class of the population. Whatever labour demands must perforce be conceded even until industry collapses. That is clear. No law can be enforced that would change this situation. Labour has a monopoly, and the very best that society can hope for is moderation of demands. The farmers, by acting together militantly, could starve Canada, including the labouring man, into paying any price for food they chose to dictate. There is no particular trick about that. Any jackass, wielding a bludgeon and flourishing a shooting iron, can take the purse from an unarmed manor woman. But we all thought that the new world was to function on the principle of the "square deal"—justice to all.

$$\blacklozenge$$

I say to the labouring man, in all seriousness: "Don't rock the boat." The industrial situation in Canada is in the flux. Many industries are face to face with far-reaching changes in production; in many cases complete mechanical re-organization. Owing to labour unrest, those who could go full steam ahead, hesitate to enter into contracts, not knowing what wage demands may at any time be made upon them. The whole international industrial system is in process of re-organization. No manufacturer knows what tomorrow may bring forth. It is a period for caution. Seriously, is this the opportune time to enforce your demands—to declare war? Because, that is what it means. You have gained much in recent years and you will gain more, but give your country a chance to take breath and settle down after the recent exertion. You can afford to wait awhile until industry finds its bearings and can discuss the future with you intelligently. Be patriotic!

There is also a word of warning due to the crack-brained anarchist. . . . I am not going to insult the decent, self-respecting worker by classing him with you, so far, an infinitesimally small, if blatant, quantity in Canada. Our environment is uncongenial to you. Your very profession of faith renders you impervious to argument. You would fail to understand. You are generally the product of the slums of European cities—the issue of feeble-minded parents. That is your misfortune and, to some extent, your justification. Your sort is having its fling in Russia today, murdering, pillaging and destroying. This present terror may wipe off the face of the earth cities, towns, arts and industries of that unfortunate country. But any of these vandals who escape death by violence or well-merited starvation will live to realize that the Soul of Russia—in the safe custody of the "man on the land"—can never be destroyed. It cannot even be polluted for long by contact with this degenerate scum of humanity—the worthy offspring of that frenzied, body and mind destroying, industrialism which the modern world falls down and worships abjectly as the greatest of national achievements. The real Russia goes on her way imperturbably. In her primitive strength she will live and prosper even without cities and towns and industry and capital and labour. Canada is precisely the same kind of country, but with this important difference, that we have an enlightened and aggressive agricultural population here which outnumbers all other classes combined. Take that lesson to heart.

Upon the employer I would urge, as his patriotic duty at this time, an immediate and careful investigation into any grievances of his employees. Get together! Anticipate the claims of labour. The wages you pay, and conditions of employment, must compare favourably with those prevailing elsewhere. If they do not, and you cannot now correct them and live—and there are many cases of this sort—call your employees together and take them into your confidence. Then you have done your full duty. The day of splendid isolation on the part of the employer is gone. The new day is dawning.

EIGHT

The Single Tax Controversy

THIS VOLUME WOULD be incomplete without some reference to the single tax system. The sentiment in favour of the adoption of single taxation is undoubtedly growing throughout Canada. The organized farmers have definitely incorporated the policy in their platform and the system numbers amongst its adherents many able and influential men. The issue is distinctly and emphatically before the public in this country and it, therefore, merits the most serious consideration.

I have for years honestly attempted to master, at least, the fundamentals of the system and have diligently read a great deal of the extensive literature available. Single taxation is very evidently less of an economic than a social system. It is heralded as the only comprehensive, all embracing, and just scheme of taxation. It is also claimed that its adoption would be followed by the elimination of poverty through the more equal distribution of wealth.

The scheme, broadly speaking, is to collect taxes on the site or rental value of land only, and not on improvements, to impose special taxation on unearned increment in land and to abolish all other forms of taxation including import duties. As a taxation proposal, pure and simple, it has undoubted merits. But the point, of course, is that the land tax would be so large that it would practically absorb almost entirely its annual rental value. In other words, it would appear to be practically equivalent to confiscation of all land for the public benefit. The issue is almost wholly one of degree and the extraordinary feature about the case is that one is never able to pin the single taxer down to anything concrete on that subject. Statistical information is readily available, on which calculations could be based, forecasting in detail almost the exact financial operation of such a plan, if consistently carried out, but such calculations are conspicuous by their absence. The high priests of single tax ask the public to take almost everything on trust. This attitude is unfair.

Opinions will be divided as to the morality of the wholesale confiscation of land. Why a citizen who, for the time being, has his savings invested in land, should have it confiscated, or even partly confiscated, while another, who left his money in the bank or put it into railway shares, remains in undisturbed possession of his property, is difficult to see. The single tax advocate hastens to explain that the ownership of land is immoral and that, therefore, no wrong is done by the State in taking its own. But that fine-spun theory does not eliminate the hardship to the absolutely innocent individual who happens to be a land owner for the time being.

The literature on the subject is generally most obscure and disappointing. We are told that with the whole burden of taxation against the land, rents would not increase. Authority after authority (mostly obsolete) is quoted on that point. To the ordinary mind, the first and obvious effect of an increase in taxation of land would be a corresponding increase in rents, and the burden would be automatically transferred. That happens now every day in our larger cities, and also in connection with farm tenancy. The tax is simply part of the overhead cost of administering real property and is recovered in the rental charge.

◆

In spite of the fact that the single tax theory has been urged, in season and out of season, for more than a generation, no country has as yet adopted it completely. In fact, Canada, particularly the West, has perhaps gone farther in this direction than any other country and sometimes with unhappy results. These, we are told, are due to the fact that the system has not been applied in its entirety. Land, as a basis for taxation, is in itself an attractive proposition. It is visible and cannot be made away with. Its ownership and value may easily be ascertained. It can unquestionably be made the basis of a just taxation system. But not necessarily to the exclusion of all other sources of internal revenue.

The single taxer reserves for the State the greater part of the unearned increment on land. If you buy an acre of land for $10.00 and then sell it for $25.00, the State steps in and takes all or part of the profits. That idea has much to recommend it, but supposing it is bought for $25.00 and then foreclosed on a basis of $10? That makes an awkward situation, and there are cases of that sort every day.

We are perhaps expecting a little too much of human nature when we want a farm owner, for instance, to become wildly enthusiastic over it. He, let us suppose, was one of the early pioneers and obtained his land for nothing. He has now, by the sweat of his brow and by all sorts of hardship and self-denial, transformed his half-section of bleak prairie into a real home with waving grain fields, and flowers growing all around the comfortable homestead. Perhaps he wants to retire. He may be getting on in years or lacking in health and have no family. His land is his chief asset. He wants to sell at the best possible figure. Why should he be deprived of the fruits of his labour through the operation of a confiscating increment tax? God knows that he deserves every cent he will ever get out of that farm. I have pioneered myself in two provinces and my sympathy goes out to that man. We can't ever do enough for him. He has done more for the public than the public will ever, or can ever, do for him. What right has the single taxer to maintain that the increased value of this land is entirely due to the community which, as a matter of fact, played a comparatively small part in its enhanced value? It is sheer exaggeration.

———————◆———————

The very first element in taxation must necessarily be the ability of the State to collect. On imports we collect taxes in advance. As to tax on income, the citizen and all he owns is liable. On a land tax, the land only is the security. Governments cannot carry on the public services and pay for them in town lots. They must have real money. Here is the first difficulty. Urban land values all over Canada, and particularly in Western Canada, are largely fictitious just now, and probably will be for many years to come. A single tax, as heavy as such a tax would necessarily be, would not lend itself very readily to raising revenue out of non-productive town lots.

Let us take a case in point and see how it would work out. The Town of Chilliwack in British Columbia has a population of 1,600 souls. It covers an area of 1,040 acres. It could comfortably take care of its population on 160 acres. That would give about half an acre to each family. We may, therefore, take it for granted that about 880 acres is held speculatively—not necessarily by people who have bought property at a song, and now, with consummate greed, stand by to see Chilliwack grow into a city by the efforts of others, when they will calmly sell and depart with their ill-gotten gains. More likely the unfortunate owners of this property have paid ridiculous prices for it and would be glad to sell at any time for a mere fraction of what the investment had cost them originally. Most of these speculative owners have probably by this time abandoned their property rather than continue paying the heavy municipal taxes.

However, under a consistent single tax plan, the problem would face the Minister of Finance to collect from the Town of Chilliwack and sum of, at least, $143,000, made up as follows:

1. Dominion Tax based on total estimated Federal expenditure of 300 millions, being at the rate of $37.50 per head of population in Canada. Chilliwack has 1,600 inhabitants.	$60,000.00
2. In lieu of Provincial Income Tax now levied, not less than	6,000.00
3. In lieu of Municipal Tax now levied, approximately	77,000.00
	$143,000.00

The total land assessment of Chilliwack is $975,000, of which doubtless not fifty per cent could be realized at any price, having in view the present tax liability to the municipality. What would be the condition of this town under a rate of taxation amounting to fifteen per cent of the present high assessed value of all land? The State would soon own it all.

It may be argued that the example cited is not an average one. Possibly, but it is not by any means an isolated one. Hundreds of urban municipalities throughout the West, and doubtless many in the East, are in the same, or even in a much worse position. A taxation system of this sort must necessarily be susceptible to general application. If it falls down in even one locality it is unworkable. We cannot enforce it in the city of Montreal, where it might apply, and adopt some other system in the smaller towns.

<hr />

It seems evident that if the single tax system will work anywhere, it is in the taxation of agricultural lands. But the single tax enthusiast tells us that the intention is to make the urban centres carry the main burden and deal gently with the farmer. That simply cannot be done. As a policy it would be dishonest. We are, therefore, face to face with the uncomfortable fact that the farmer, whose main asset is necessarily his land, cannot hope to escape heavy taxation, whereas the city man, whose assets may be, and frequently are, confined to stocks and bonds and other business investments, would escape taxation entirely. He may pay indirectly, but that supposition is much too theoretical for practical discussion. If rents are not to be advanced, how would he pay?

We are told that the proposal is to sweep away all other forms of taxation and concentrate the levying of taxes, for public revenues of all sorts, upon the land. Then it naturally follows that the greatest land-owning class in Canada, viz., the farmer, must look forward to contributing a greater proportion of taxes than he is doing under our present dual system. I say "dual system" advisedly, for we now have, in the West, at least, practically a system of single tax as far as provincial and municipal revenues are concerned. Federal revenue is, of course, raised by means of import duties and income tax and in various other ways. The single taxer then advances the argument that his system automatically involves a change in our fiscal policy—that it means free trade, and that the farmer, by virtue of being able to purchase his goods in a cheaper market, could well afford to pay a higher tax on his land. The real point, therefore, seems to be, whether the farmer would in the end, contribute more under a tax upon his land only, than he now does with a nominal land tax, but labouring under the handicap of a "tariff-for-revenue" system with its indirect burden. In other words, the main question apparently is not one of single tax at all, but of fiscal policy. It is a pity that the two should be mixed. It beclouds public understanding of a very important subject. What we want is straight and clear thinking: facts and not fads.

One never ceases to wonder what species of hypnotic influence the single tax enthusiasts have exercised on the farmers to enlist their support. The farmer of Canada should be the governor on the engine of public opinion and the brake on hasty and ill-considered public action. As the great land-owner, this becomes his natural role and responsibility, as it has in every country on earth since the dawn of civilization. The apostles of single tax should make it abundantly clear on what basis they claim the support of the farmer. We want less oratory and froth, and more facts and figures, which may be easily digested and understood.

◆

Even in its application in urban centres, there are some very serious objections to the principle of the single land tax, which I shall only touch upon lightly. We have spent large sums of money in Canada on propaganda work in connection with town planning, the object being to bring about such reforms in urban administration that our towns and cities will become more healthful and more beautiful and altogether more desirable as places of residence. It is difficult to imagine any movement more promising in its scope and effect.

The very foundation of intelligent town planning is to ensure that houses are not jammed up one against the other in the residential areas, but that each residence has a generous site for garden and ornamental purposes. This has been distinctly discouraged in our western towns as the direct result of the limited municipal single tax system. The tax, being based on land value only, it follows that the man who builds on two lots of twenty-five feet frontage each, which just gives sufficient room for the average small house, will pay only one half the taxes his neighbour pays who devotes an additional two lots to lawn and garden and is thus a public benefactor.

Another effect would be the gradual elimination of the individual home and the introduction on a large scale of apartment and tenement buildings. Obviously, with a very heavy tax on the ground, the object would be to crowd as many families upon a given area of land as possible. This practice is now very common, but would be inevitable with heavy ground rents or taxes. Surely, we could not contemplate such a development with equanimity! Our cities would become as congested as they are in Europe, with lasting injury to the health and well-being of our children and ourselves.

It is also clear that the burden of taxation would automatically be reduced upon the principal streets of our cities, with their imposing office buildings and stores, and would be increased correspondingly upon inferior business properties, which even now cannot stand very many additional burdens. This would mean that the most affluent citizens would apparently be relieved of heavy taxation, to the detriment of those not so well able to contribute.

◆

Before leaving this subject, I want to comment briefly on the question of the attitude of the State towards the non-resident land owner. This much abused individual receives scant sympathy. Every possible method is used to make his burden intolerable. Frequently he is not a resident of the community wherein he owns land and, therefore, is not a political factor. The single taxer frankly desires to make his position untenable. While the problem of the unoccupied land, title for which has passed from the Crown, is to some extent a general one, I shall deal more particularly with the Western situation, which seems to worry many of our ardent reformers.

The Western provinces have now passed legislation dealing with the subject. The "Wild Land Tax" has a two-fold object in view. First and foremost, to raise revenue. Secondly, to promote the settlement of unimproved lands. Of course, the taxation of unoccupied lands holds out great attractions to those who are responsible for raising the necessary revenue to defray the expense of our provincial public services. The owners, in most cases, are not there to raise objections. And, better still, they are not even there to vote against the Government, which may indulge in sweet dreams of the happy state of legislators if all revenue could be raised by taxing absentees!

To the personal knowledge of the writer, a very large proportion of the unoccupied land in Western Canada, outside Hudson's Bay Co., railway and school lands, is not held by speculators, but by men who came to Canada, generally from the United States, to buy farms with the full intention of settling on them as soon as they could disentangle themselves from their home interests. This sometimes takes years to do. Why did these men buy land in Western Canada before they were able to settle on it? Because they had no intention of making any move until they knew they could get satisfactorily placed elsewhere. Therefore, they had to secure land before they even attempted to sell out in their old homes, also forestalling any prohibitive increases in the price that might afterwards take place. This large army of absentee land owners is now contemptuously classed as "speculators," simply because they exercised ordinary business foresight.

To regard them as enemies of the country seems a very far-fetched theory. They are now bearing the burden of normal taxes and, in addition, are paying the extra "wild land" tax, while the unoccupied land they own is being put to beneficial use by the settlers in the neighbourhood, for grazing purposes. Are not these men really benefactors? I confess they have my full sympathy. Their lot is not an enviable one. We persist in ranting about the "settlement of our vacant lands." Let us be honest and admit that the Provinces tax them now because they need the money and need it badly.

There is, of course, the case of the vacant town or city lot to be considered. But why waste time on elaborating taxation schemes for that class of landed property? No one wants it. The burden of municipal taxation is now almost intolerable and the title to the greater part of out-lying property of that class will doubtless pass, or has already passed, to the various municipalities, through the ex-pedient of tax sales. Inside vacant lots of greater value lie idle be-cause the demand for buildings is not there. No sane man would carry an investment of that sort in an undeveloped state, in the face of a large annual tax bill, if there was the slightest possibility of making it revenue producing. As a general rule, the unfortunate owner of this class of property is quite sufficiently punished by the very reason of his ownership, without devising special means of in-flicting further penalties.

The whole problem of the settlement of our vacant farm lands in the West is not to be solved by any iniquitous system of con-fiscatory taxation such as is clearly in evidence now. It is rather a case for promoting general colonization and for bringing intending settlers and absentee land-owners together, so that a sale may be conveniently effected.

NINE

Industry and Tariff

THERE CAN BE NO possible argument against a national policy of encouragement of the industrial development of Canada, although there may be widely divergent opinions as to the precise method of doing so. A nation is composed of individuals with varied ambitions and preferences in the way of occupations. If they cannot find sufficient scope for their talent at home, they emigrate to countries where they can, which is a loss to the State. There is, however, as above stated, ample room for argument as to the most efficient and fair methods of extending encouragement to industry, and this is, unquestionably, the greatest conundrum that faces Canada today.

Every country presents peculiar problems of its own in this respect. Canada's industrial section is now largely confined to Ontario and Quebec. These Provinces, unfortunately, are not generously endowed with the natural resources that form the raw materials of industry. They do not produce a single ton of coal. The Nova Scotia coal comes up by water only as far as Montreal. Ontario, therefore, is absolutely dependent upon the United States for every pound of coal consumed, domestic as well as industrial. To make matters worse, we have no great iron deposits available in Eastern Canada which can be developed profitably. Such a state of affairs would ordinarily make industrial development very difficult. Ontario, however, has succeeded in rendering available enormous water power, which to a limited extent, equalizes the situation. Out of the total Canadian water power of over two million horse power, now developed, Ontario has the lion's share. The per capita figures for other countries show that next to Sweden and Norway, Canada ranks the highest in developed water power according to the population. This is most satisfactory and encouraging.

The concentration of our industrial energies on the manufacture of war material and munitions during the great war has, however, opened up new possibilities for the extension of industries. Canadian manufacturers, coming into direct competition with the world, made a proud record for themselves. They demonstrated their ability to produce against all comers, in point of economy as well as quality of product. When the full story is told we shall find that our industrial leaders and our man-power are second to none in the world.

Great possibilities are looming up with regard to steel production in Canada. We have extensive deposits of magnesite in Eastern Canada which were developed during the war. Our carbon electrodes stand in the very first rank and can compete successfully with the British in point of cheapness. We also have our vast nickel deposits which are now developed to a very high standard. Under the circumstances, nothing seems to stand in the way of Canada branching into the manufacture of high quality steels. Our annual steel production has been increased from one million tons pre-war production to two and a quarter million tons. We have a few other raw materials in abundance, notably pulpwood, which are also leading to increased industrial production.

A recent industrial survey by the Canadian Census Bureau shows healthy progress. The gross value of goods made in Canada in 1917 amounted to $3,015,506,869, and the cost of material was $1,602,820,631, leaving a net value added by the process of manufacture of $1,412,686,238, or $5,449,098 more than the gross value of production in 1915.

There are special reasons why we should promote our export trade. We have enormous interest payments facing us abroad. These must be met largely by exports. But the basic principle should be that industry should be encouraged only to have Canadian labour most profitably employed. We certainly cannot afford to employ Canadian labour in making articles that the foreigner can make much cheaper than we can. It is a waste of time, energy and capital. The result of such a condition most frequently leads to capital and labour being employed in unnatural, artificial industries, when these forces could be profitably employed in developing industries natural to the country.

◆

Soon after Confederation, while Canada was young, the Government of the day in its wisdom decided to inaugurate a policy of encouragement to Canadian industry. The proposal was labelled the "National Policy" and became law after a hotly contested election. It was designed to protect infant industries and, incidentally, produce Federal revenue. This was the programme of the Conservative party. The Liberals for years denounced as iniquitous any proposal to protect industry. We should have free trade, "as they have it in England." In the fulness of time the Liberals became the "ins," in Canadian politics. But the tariff remained, except for a few spectacular but inconsiderable amendments. In fact, with the responsibilities of office, or perhaps impairment of profitable sources from which to draw the party funds, the Liberals experienced a change of heart and a "tariff for revenue only" became the party slogan. This was calculated to square the consciences of all. As above stated, the "protective" tariff of the Conservatives and the "revenue" tariff of the Liberals were precisely the same dog under a new name. Incidentally, this flagrant violation of specific pre-election promises, is perhaps the most disgraceful chapter in Canada's political history. This tariff policy, with entirely unimportant modifications, has remained in effect ever since.

I entertain grave doubts as to the wisdom of developing industry by the indirect means of an admittedly unscientific tariff. I question its efficiency, and particularly its expediency and justice. A sound industrial policy would, of course, encourage only such industries as held out reasonable expectations of getting on an export basis through proper specialization and favourable environments. To have protected Canadian industries for fifty years at the expense of the public, with the only result that the tariff has had to be increased from time to time at the bidding of these industries, show conclusively that there has been no substantial, healthy progress and that these industries are apparently less able to support themselves now than they were 50 years ago. To argue for one moment that the people of Canada, east or west, will be satisfied with such a policy is futile.

The present is a most appropriate time to take stock. The great war has entirely revolutionized the world's industrial situation. Tariff barriers were primarily justified on the plea that any country offering its workers decent wages, hours and labour conditions, could not fairly be asked to compete with other countries paying starvation wages, imposing long hours and permitting the exploitation of labour without restriction. That was plausible. We are now, however, face to face with the international emancipation of workers, leading to wages as high and hours as short as the most advanced country ever conceded to labour. Cost of living on the continent of America will be as low as in any country in Europe; perhaps lower. The burden of taxation in Europe will be enormous, comparatively speaking, which will automatically increase industrial overhead cost there. Add to this the admitted superiority of our manpower, productive and executive, and the gloomiest pessimist cannot fail to agree that we should in the future be able to compete against all comers. The German commercial menace has vanished. Japanese labour shows signs of falling in line. Canadian industries should now be able to compete in the export market on an even basis. All this has an important bearing on the fiscal issue.

◆

It is difficult to grasp the point of view of those who have guided Dominion finances since Confederation. We started with a policy of out-and-out protection. Needless to say, we never had protection as a consistent fiscal system. We don't apparently even realize what the word implies. A protective system creates a tariff wall high enough to keep foreign products out. With necessary modifications, this is the principle involved. Hence, it cannot be depended upon

for revenue. Also, it clearly contemplates a periodical expert investigation of protected industries so as to promptly reduce, or entirely
remove, the measure of protection as soon as the infant industry
shows its ability to live without artificial stimulant or upon reduced
rations. The whole drift of a true protective system is, of course, towards free trade. I leave it to the reader to judge to what extent we
have had "protection" in Canada, as a consistent policy! We have
been saddled with a corrupt and pernicious fiscal system that cannot be defended on any grounds of public interest, that rests on no
sound economic principles, that is simply an ugly hybrid, neither
fowl nor fish.

◆

As a revenue collecting and producing system, our tariff appears to
have little to recommend it, beyond the fact that it successfully fools
the taxpayer. Politically, that is, of course, a tremendous asset. As
far as the individual citizen is concerned it is an unmitigated
nuisance. Any small purchase made outside the boundaries of Canada involves a visit to a custom house and the filling out of in-
numerable forms and complying with other red tape and perhaps in
the end the payment of only a trifling amount, frequently much less
than the cost of collecting it. This perhaps is a small objection. As to
the cost of collection, it can hardly be urged that the present tariff is
a shining example of efficiency and economy. In 1915 we collected
in customs duties 76 million dollars and spent 3¾ millions on doing
it. A direct tax could, of course, have been collected at a much
smaller cost, once an efficient service for the purpose was organized.

Is the burden of taxation equally distributed under the present
system? It is almost unnecessary to waste time on this phase of the
question. It must be abundantly clear to the lowest intellect that
nothing could be more unfair and erratic than the taxation feature
of the present tariff. No one knows what any individual pays.
When this has been said, practically everything necessary is said.
That it is glaringly unjust is, however, self evident. The rich
bachelor, unless he buys expensive cigars or wines, pays compara-

tively little. The father of a large family is necessarily heavily taxed, as his family would generally consume more imported commodities.

But the vilest feature of the whole system is that the presence of a protective tariff raises the prices of home made commodities, so that a tax is automatically levied whether such commodity is made at home or imported from abroad. The only difference is that in the case of the domestic product, the tax is paid to the protected industry and not to the Government. Who can make head or tail of this maze of indirect taxation, partly for the benefit of Government and partly for private enterprise? Can it be intelligently considered at all? If not, how can it be justified?

From a standpoint of fair play and equity—and, I take it, that those principles must be fundamental to any efficient taxation scheme—a system of "tariff-for-revenue-only," except when confined strictly to luxuries and perhaps to a few commodities of universal consumption, as it is in Great Britain, is apparently about as intelligent and just as would be a policy of levying special taxes on all baldheaded men. Even for such a tax, the wily protectionist would doubtless find a justification. He would probably maintain that the ulterior motive was to promote the luxuriant growth of hair on shiny Canadian domes! He is far more plausible than the dense, stupid "revenue" tariff advocate, with his lame and impotent kindergarten arguments.

◆

It is instructive to see just how far Canada's hybrid tariff promotes the development of her natural resources. As usual, the best evidence is the concrete case. For obvious reasons, I shall mention no names.

A certain large coal mine is capitalized at some millions of dollars. It has a record of failure behind it and has probably never paid a dividend, at least, not during recent years. The shareholders are sick and tired of the investment. Some time ago it was decided to have an expert examination made in order to ascertain what was wrong and whether it could be corrected. The report was to the effect that the machinery and equipment of the mine were antiquated and that no relief could be hoped for, until modern appliances were available so that coal could be brought to the surface at a reduced cost per ton.

This was bad news, as there was very little chance of inducing the shareholders to put further capital into a venture which had proved so disappointing. However, a competent engineer went to work and made an estimate of the cost involved. It amounted in round figures to somewhat over $250,000. A carefully prepared case was then made and submitted to certain influential shareholders, residing in the United States, in an endeavour to obtain the necessary capital to promote more efficient and economical operations in the mines. After untold trouble, a tentative agreement was reached and the company approached the customs authorities to ascertain what tax Canada was going to impose on the new equipment required. My impression is that it exceeded $30,000. The facts were communicated to the shareholders interested, with the result that they refused to continue negotiations. The mine today is still running on the old, extravagant basis, with obsolete and insufficient machinery and equipment. This is how we promote industry and the development of our resources in Canada by means of a protective tariff.

On every side industry is penalized by prohibitive duties on the very machinery and implements that form the basis of its existence. Whether these duties are levied for "revenue" or not, is immaterial. That the practice is inconsistent and ruinous should be clear to any mind which has grasped the first principles of political economy.

Furthermore, what is the raw material in one industry is the finished article in another. Thus we find most protected industries paying import duties on their raw materials as well as upon machinery. In some cases, the amounts so paid very nearly absorb the total amount of any protection afforded. We have nursed into life a complicated system, which defies comprehension. Experts only can tell the net amount of protection an industry receives. I know one industry that receives nominal protection amounting to 35 per cent while its net protective margin is less than 10 per cent. What we give with one hand, we take away with the other.

———————◆———————

Precisely what are we trying to accomplish through our present protective tariff policy? Was it the expectation of the authors of this legislation that half a century after its passage the tariff would be higher than ever? Is it the intention that for all time to come, a privileged class is to be licensed to collect from Canadian consumers up to 45 per cent of the cost elsewhere of articles of every day use, thus keeping the cost of living in Canada permanently on an artificially high level? If so, what is the ultimate goal to which such an extraordinary policy is intended to lead us? If not, what is the time limit, if there is a time or any other limit, and what are we waiting for in the case of some notorious cases of looting the public under the shadow of our protective tariff? These seem very simple questions that honest advocates of this system might fairly be asked to answer categorically. It is scarcely to be supposed that our policy is merely to drift aimlessly on the fiscal sea. There surely must be an objective of some sort. If we could once ascertain what this objective is, we should be in a much better position to intelligently determine whether or not the price we are now paying for industrial development is worth while.

We are told that our industries would be swept out of existence over night if the present tariff barrier were removed, as they could not compete with those of the United States and Great Britain. It is asserted that if we had a population as great as the former country to cater for, all would be well. We could then specialize as they do there and manufacture at lower costs. That argument looks very reasonable and plausible to those who properly appreciate the tremendous bearing which output has on cost of production and wide markets on economical specialization.

Let us, however, see how it has actually worked out in Canada under the blighting influence of a tariff created trade monopoly. Our boot and shoe industry is one of the greatest in Canada. It has powerful capital and large organization behind it. We have for many years enjoyed absolute free access for boots and shoes in the market of the United States. There is, and has been, nothing whatever to prevent Canadian industry organizing to compete in that market with that of Massachusetts. Yet, the Canadian boot and shoe industry now comes forward and tells us that it has been unable to expand and that it is barely making a living and that, if the present enormous duties upon imports of boots and shoes into this country are removed, the industry will quickly die. We find then that apparently a wide market does not lead to success in this industry. When we endeavour to ascertain the nature of the obstacles in the way, we are vaguely apologetically informed that Boston is the great leather centre, that large capital is available there for industrial expansion, that the highest trade and executive skill is at the command of industry in the New England States, that, as a matter of fact, it is quite hopeless to enter the field in competition with an industry so favourably located and strongly entrenched.

The inference apparently is that we must wait until we have a hundred million people in Canada, when we can create our own Boston and our own leather centre. But by that time, they will probably have five hundred million people in the United States and a Boston trade centre ten times as powerful and well organized as it is now. We find then that as far as this particular industry is concerned we have just been living in a fool's paradise. We have for half a century, stupidly and stolidly, taxed every man, woman and child in Canada a dollar or two upon every pair of boots they have purchased, in the vain hope of building up a great industry in Canada, which it is now clearly shown could not be done. Our boot and shoe trade, candidly admitting the complete and ghastly failure of fifty years of protection to assist it to attain a self supporting basis, now calmly proposes that this industry shall, presumably for all time to come, be placed in the position of a pensioner upon the Canadian people! Will any responsible political leader become a party to such arrangement?

Strong pressure is being brought to bear by Canadian farmers in favour of the free admission of agricultural implements. To counteract this propaganda, an organization, acting on behalf of Canadian farm implement manufacturers, recently published elaborate statistics to show that a certain standard self-binder, manufactured in Canada, is actually sold at a lower price in the Canadian West than a similar implement, made in the United States, can be purchased for at corresponding points in the westerly part of that country. Some of the prices quoted are, by the way, not quite convincing. To clearly prove that the Canadian product is, as a matter of fact, superior to the American, it is gravely asserted that in the foreign market, where they compete on an even basis, dealers will readily pay a premium for the Canadian article. This is most reassuring and encouraging information. And yet, this very advertisement is published and paid for presumably with the sole object of convincing the people of Canada that without a high tariff wall against the United States, our farm implement industry must perish miserably! By their own showing, it is apparently lack of mere salesmanship that prevents the Canadian from beating the American out in this market without any protection whatsoever, seeing that we admittedly have a superior article at a lower price! Perhaps what our implement industry really wants is free admission of raw materials and a fair field. But human nature is so selfish. Any tariff manipulation that will put a ring fence around the home market and thus create an opportunity to arbitrarily levy higher prices and, at the same time, to decrease selling cost and effort, will, of course, always be welcome. It is a special privilege grudgingly relinquished. We apparently pay a premium on commercial indolence and stagnation in Canada.

The whole tariff controversy is very much before the public at present and the press of Canada is naturally taking sides according to conviction. The time is opportune for constructive deliberation and the reading public eagerly scans the columns of the press for new arguments pro and con. One is struck with the poverty of the protectionist argument. Some influential journals frankly state that those favouring protection are apparently in the majority and as we have majority rule in Canada, the agrarian point of view cannot at present be given effect. The farmers of Canada are in the majority and by acting together could cause legislation to be passed providing that all taxes should be paid by the other classes; and that the farmers should be entirely relieved of taxation and should, on the contrary, receive a bonus from the public funds. Two or three religious denominations might similarly act together and decree that all taxation should be levied exclusively on the Presbyterians and Baptists. We are, however, largely governed by unwritten laws. We cannot with impunity create privileged classes and make one class of the community hewers of wood and drawers of water for another.

Another paper laboriously collected statistics of customs receipts west of Lake Superior and by comparing them with the total receipts found that they were so inconsiderable that the West apparently had no tariff grievance at all, when almost everyone should know that the bulk of western imports enter through the Ports of Montreal, Toronto and other large trading centres in Eastern Canada and from there are distributed throughout the country.

The soundest argument against drastic tariff reform that has been advanced so far seems to be that by virtue of the National Policy certain vested rights were created in Canada and much capital invested in industry in good faith and that this capital is entitled to consideration in any fiscal readjustment that may be made. Also, that any violent changes in our tariff law would be followed by serious consequences. These two points cannot be evaded. They are not arguments in favour of the principle of protection, but rather a plea to respect legitimate property rights which cannot be thrust aside. It is a pity that so little trouble has been taken to mould intelligent public opinion on this subject. The western farmer has not been made to understand clearly that the change from one fiscal policy to another must of necessity be made by easy stages and on a well conceived plan. Common decency and common prudence would dictate such a course. Industries to be deprived, or partly deprived, of protection hitherto accorded them by the law of the land must be given every opportunity to adjust themselves to the new conditions. Whether the policy itself has been right or wrong has nothing whatever to do with this phase of the question. The farmer can be made to see clearly the wisdom of sympathetic aid to Canada's industries during any such transition period. No deserving industry should be seriously damaged.

It seems to me that the time has come when we are entitled to definite assurances on this important subject from whatever political party that is ready to espouse protection in Canada as a permanent trade or fiscal policy. The old story is out of date. The people are sick and tired of indeterminate policy. We want concrete definition. For instance, how many years does it take for an "infant" industry to mature? We have seen that half a century is too short a period to allow. The "infant" is still in the nursery and is apparently a good example of arrested development.

◆

It has been well said that the tariff is a local question. Just how local, few of us realize. For instance, let us suppose that the City of Toronto is ambitious to make ploughs. It can only be done under a protective tariff. Every farmer throughout the Dominion is then taxed, either for the benefit of the Treasury or directly for the benefit of this industry, according as to whether he imports his plough or buys one made in Toronto. Who is the beneficiary? Traders in Toronto, until competition becomes keener, enjoy increased business by reason of the larger population brought to the city by this plough industry. Real estate there increases in value. Farmers in the vicinity get perhaps a little better price for their products in the Toronto market than they did before. But what about the farmer in Prince Edward Island or in Alberta? Is he in the very least interested in this Toronto industry? If not, why should he be taxed to maintain it? Unless, indeed, Toronto can show that her citizens are directly contributing towards the welfare of Alberta or P.E.I. farmers. It seems unjust.

It would appear as if some system could be worked out, in the event of the protective principle being perpetuated in Canada's fiscal policy, of appraising the respective value of industries to individual communities and to the country at large. Some contribution might then be demanded from the city or the county, or both, within which a protected industry is located. If it is worth the while of a Canadian farmer in Nova Scotia to pay a large indirect tax to develop certain industries in Ontario or Quebec cities, it surely is worth the while of the property owners immediately benefited by the location and expansion of such industries, to contribute directly towards their development, just as a western town would do in offering a bonus for the location of an industry. If not, what is the object of the protective tariff? If the population and property owners in and around industrial centres do not benefit, who does? And if they do, why not place a fair share of the burden where it properly belongs? Let us, at least, be consistent.

If it could be clearly shown that a certain industry could be successfully developed in Canada by being assured the home market for a certain period of years, it might be quite feasible, by a system of import licenses, to control imports of the article to be manufactured, also, of course, controlling the domestic selling price of the said article as they aim to do in Australia under their fiscal system. This would be simple and efficient.

There are other methods of assisting industry without the intervention of the protective tariff. A simple plan would be to bonus an industry until such time as its earnings, on *bona fide* capital only, exceeded a reasonable percentage. We would, at least, know exactly what we were doing and could intelligently control our actions. Under the present system, we merely license private interests to levy toll on the public without supervision. We "farm out" our taxes as they do in China.

It will, of course, be objected that the country would never stand for a plan of direct bonus payments. Why not? Is it because we insist upon being fooled and befuddled? Is the taxpayer of Canada so silly that he cannot be trusted to know exactly how much he is to pay and what the money is to be used for? The world has decreed that the day of secret diplomacy is over. We want clear daylight let in upon all our public transactions. The argument that the country could not stand the financial strain of direct bonus payment is, of course, utterly absurd. Someone assuredly pays it now and if the industrial development of Canada is a great, national necessity, as we are assured it is, why, in the name of common sense, should taxation in aid of this vital national objective be levied solely and exclusively on purchasers of ploughs, spades, etc. The tax should in all fairness be equally distributed over the whole population.

Under any fiscal system this country may adopt, no sound argument can be advanced in opposition to absolutely protecting Canadian producers against those of other countries attempting to exploit Canada as a slaughter market. The "dumping clause" in the present tariff legislation is designed to deal with this evil in respect of which Canadian consumers, as a rule, are very superficially informed. That a real grievance exists is beyond all doubt. A producer in the United States, let us say, finds it necessary to manufacture a minimum quantity of goods in order to keep his production costs below a certain figure. His home market will not absorb his entire output and, in order not to demoralize prices in the most valuable outlet for his goods, he adopts the expedient of shipping his unsaleable surplus to a foreign market to be sold at whatever prices he can realize, frequently at figures below actual cost of manufacture. This practice is much more common than the public realizes. Obviously, the Canadian producer cannot compete under such conditions for any length of time and his industry runs the danger of being ruined. Once having destroyed competition, the foreign exporter would, of course, be able to exact his regular prices in our market. The advantage of low prices to the consumer is, therefore, only temporary. It is also conceivable that a "dumping" policy might systematically be resorted to in order to oust a competing industry from a convenient foreign market such as Canada. Canadian consumers cannot fairly object to paying a living price for manufactured products and enlightened public opinion would doubtless support any Government in providing drastic legislation authorizing the absolute confiscation of shipments into Canada of goods invoiced at prices below the current selling values in the country where such goods originated. Canadian industries are absolutely entitled to a fair field in our own country, which by no means implies detriment to others. The principle involved in the restrictions suggested, is entirely different from that underlying the imposition of a prohibitory import duty.

◆

At the very outset, let us clearly realize that the real problem facing Canada lies in reconciling the diametrically opposed views and interests of two great geographical sections, divided for all time to come by an enormous unproductive waste. These two sections have little in common, commercially, and are held together by sentiment only: a link which, in view of the rapid settlement of the Western portion by people who have no knowledge of, or natural sentimental interest in, the Eastern section, is bound to become weaker year by year.

It is a significant fact that in that part of Canada lying west of Lake Superior, only 34 per cent of the population is of Canadian origin. Approximately 29 per cent came from Great Britain and 37 per cent hail from the United States and foreign countries. There lies the problem. The settler from Kansas or Idaho neither knows nor cares any more about Hamilton or Toronto than the Torontonian does about Lincoln and Leavenworth. They are merely terms, more or less familiar in school days and frequently not even that. To ask him to contribute to and wax enthusiastic over the industrial development of these cities, is absurd. This is the situation. It is a somewhat unpleasant situation. But nothing is gained by ignoring it as our public men are fond of doing.

To further complicate matters, the uncomfortable fact stares one in the face that while the West can do much for the East in the way of supplying markets for industrial products, the East, having its own agriculture, can do practically nothing in return for the West, which is on an export basis. It is, therefore, an almost wholly one-sided situation, as far as any suggestion of compromise on the tariff is concerned. This fact should also be carefully pondered.

Now, a word on the most pernicious feature of the whole controversy, namely, the seeming utter inability of the East to recognize the situation. The writer, though essentially a Westerner, is bound by every sentimental tie to Eastern Canada. His sole desire is to present the problem as fairly and impartially as this sentimental leaning will permit him, believing that unless the situation is recognized before the West is politically powerful enough to impose its views on the rest of Canada, the breach will be wide and serious, and the ultimate end will be fierce sectional warfare. Nothing could be more deplorable than such an eventuality. When the tariff question is discussed by Eastern public men, their attitude almost invariably is that the West must sink its selfish desires and make some sacrifices in the common cause and thus repay the East for all it has done for the West. I know of no more tactless and irritating argument.

◆

Let us clear the air and be precise. What sacrifices has the East made for the West? I know of none. If the Canadian Pacific and other railways were built as philanthropic enterprises and generous gifts from the East to the West, as many Easterners fondly imagine, the record of the discussions in Parliament at the time bear no evidence of any such benevolent intention. These enterprises were given public aid to open up the West and give it transportation for its products to tidewater and thus provide markets for Eastern manufactured products and to comply with the agreement under which British Columbia entered Confederation. Besides, the Canadian Pacific was not built by Eastern Canada. It was chiefly financed by a huge grant of the most desirable lands of the West. As to the other lines of railway, the less said the better from that standpoint. Furthermore, at the time autonomy was granted the Western Provinces, there was a very careful accounting of every penny Canada had ever spent on the West, which was all considered in the financial settlements. We can, therefore, safely call the account square.

How much of a factor has Eastern Canada been in the colonization of the West? As has been shown, not as much as Great Britain and the United States have been, although it has done its best. More Eastern people have probably emigrated to the United States than to Western Canada. Then we have the argument that Eastern capital has financed and built up the West. The chartered bank system of Canada has unquestionably been a drawback rather than an aid to Western agricultural development. Did these banks open up in the West with the sole object of playing the role of guide, friend and philosopher to the unsophisticated granger? Their 9 per cent loans and 12 per cent dividends and bonuses sufficiently answer the question. And loan companies—to what extend were they influenced by public spirit and to what extent by nine per cent interest rates? And how many of these self-sacrificing pillars for Western agriculture would lend a dollar on Western farms prior to the year 1900? They did not come in until the West had demonstrated its ability to pay interest and furnish reliable security for principal, a time long after United States and British capital had invested largely in our mortgage securities, with their high interest yield.

The metalliferous mining development of the West was financed almost entirely by British and United States capital; the coal mines largely by Eastern Canada. Our lumbering enterprises were almost wholly indebted to Great Britain for their capital, and most of our industrial concerns were financed locally. Eastern wholesalers have, of course, opened branches to extend their trade and many misguided Easterners have speculated in Western lands, sometimes unsuccessfully. This is the whole story.

At any rate, one cannot create sentimental obligations out of ordinary, cold-blooded business transactions. Eastern capital has gone West, and will continue to be invested there, just as long as that country can pay a higher rate of interest and give as sound security as competing fields. This is, and very properly, the investor's point of view.

I must repeat that I have, personally, nothing but the kindliest feelings towards Eastern Canada, but I conceive it to be my duty to sound the note of warning, and counsel our public men to drop all this pernicious cant, and face cold facts. From a point of view of sound public administration, no section of a community has any right to expect economic sacrifices from another merely on a plea of sentiment, except during periods of grave national crises, such as the recent war. On this occasion the West did, at least, its full duty.

Let us at once honestly admit that the West owes the East nothing that can be calculated in dollars and cents. During many weary years, the West has submitted to a severe fiscal handicap, for which the East could not give an adequate *quid pro quo*. By these sacrifices the West has contributed to the building up of great industries and financial institutions east of Lake Superior, with the incidental creation of a better market for the Eastern farmer and of high land values in Eastern cities.

It is scarcely worth while to answer the silly argument that if the West will loyally assist the East to build up its industries, some day there will be markets available there for Western agricultural produce. In the first place, Eastern Canada has a sufficient area of agricultural lands to amply take care of any farm produce, outside of wheat, that might be required in her own territory through any industrial expansion that is likely to occur. And to the West, of course, it is immaterial whether she sells her wheat in Toronto or in Liverpool, as the world price is fixed in the latter market. Secondly, if the West, with its enormous agricultural areas, had to depend upon such a restricted market, its future would be desperate indeed. Canada is so overwhelmingly agricultural that local markets for the leading products of our farms will always be a forlorn hope.

◆

A distinguished ex-Finance Minister, who should know better, recently stated, on the floor of the House, that he was unalterably opposed to dealing with the tariff through a commission. He held that this responsibility rested on the Finance Minister. He is, of course, technically, entirely wrong. Fiscal responsibility rests, first, on the Cabinet of the day, and secondly, on Parliament for giving legislative effect to the budget. This, however, is mere sophistry—political camouflage.

What he really pleads for is inefficient administration or corruption, or both. This stickler for individual ministerial responsibility evidently wants the tariff to remain as the principal issue in party politics, so that both sides may continue to befog and bedevil the voter with glittering generalities and high sounding phrases, while the protected interests are quietly pulling the strings behind the scenes. He virtually pleads for free opportunity on the part of the "machine" of politely blackmailing the industries of Canada for campaign funds, in return for which the grateful party in power may confer upon them the privilege of looting the consumer—that is, the voter. He pleads, in fact, for the *status quo*—the good, old, rotten system that has been tried and found wanting. He is almost precisely five years behind the times. He really should wake up!

I cannot resist the temptation to "tell tales." This one has a point to it. Some years ago I appeared officially before this same gentleman's amateur "ministerial" tariff commission in behalf of the Territorial Sheep Breeders' Association. We urged the removal of the duty on coyote proof woven wire fencing so as to encourage the small flock in the West. I argued that Canada's sheep industry was vanishing and, incidentally, pointed out that the tariff as regards raw wool was, and always had been (and is today), dishonestly administered. Not a dollar had ever been collected by the Government of Canada on importations running into hundreds of millions of pounds of raw wool, although the tariff distinctly contemplated that only wools of a character *not grown in Canada* shall be free. I showed that *practically every recognized class of wool was then grown in Canada* and had been for a long time. But the wool schedules had not been revised for forty years, while history was written in sheep breeding and woollen manufacturing in this country!

Having clearly demonstrated, by speech and in writing, the screaming absurdity of the present antiquated, meaningless wool schedules and also, that even the plain letter of the existing law was being flagrantly violated, did our ex-Finance Minister and his colleagues rush frantically back to Ottawa to set this matter right? Not at all. The farmers of Canada have learned that whenever the interest of agriculture clashes with that of protected industry, the result is a foregone conclusion. The situation, of course, remained exactly as it was and—still remains. And this honourable gentleman now calmly tells us that we don't want a tariff commission!

One is willing to make every reasonable allowance for sheer ignorance. Neither the ex-Finance Minister nor his colleagues probably knew an Oxford Down sheep from a barn door. But the suspicion lurks away back in my mind that they were vastly more concerned about easy money for the manufacturer and avoiding uncomfortable complications with these importunate individuals by the simple and effective expedient of continuing to connive at the violation of both the plain letter and plain spirit of the law, than they were about promoting the sheep industry of Canada. Needless to add, the duty was not removed from our wire fencing.

Talking about sheep, perhaps this notoriously passive attitude of the State towards agriculture is the reason why, while Australia has 58 sheep per hundred acre farm; Great Britain, 52; Italy, 21; Argentina, 15; France, 13; Holland, 12. Canada has—I am really ashamed to record it—actually two (2) whole sheep for each farm of one hundred acres! And, I may add, that with the exception of New Zealand and possibly Tasmania, there is no country under the sun possessing greater natural advantages for sheep farming than Canada.

The fact is that our tariff has been framed and generally administered by statesmen whose vision has been strictly limited by Montreal on the east and Toronto on the west. If we are to have a tariff in Canada we simply *must have a tariff commission.* Two things should be absolutely removed from our tariff legislation, namely, politics, and its attending evil, corruption. Such a body would necessarily report its findings to the Finance Minister, who is responsible for procuring revenue, and whose duty it would be to give effect to its recommendations as fast as circumstances permitted. It would also act as a bulwark between the Government and industry. Its reports should, however, be submitted to Parliament for its information. The principle should be clearly laid down that the business transactions of any industry, subsidized by the consumers of Canada, cannot be considered confidential. We must have clear daylight on our tariff beneficiaries.

At any rate, whatever vestige of the old tariff ultimately remains in force, it must be administered on a business basis, and protected industries must be given to understand that they must make good within a reasonable period of years or they had better direct their activities into other channels. Canada cannot afford to carry industrial pensioners on her pay list for any unlimited period. Protection must be based solely on the ascertained necessity of any industry which apparently has a reasonable chance to succeed under our conditions. Paying four dollars for two-dollar woollen garments in a cold country, will, as a permanent proposition, appeal to no considerable section of community.

◆

Those who have followed my reflections up to this point, will doubtless conclude that the situation is somewhat desperate; that the attitude of the West, on the subject of tariff, is uncompromising to the extent that nothing short of a complete reversal of Canada's present fiscal policy would prove satisfactory. This at once brings us face to face with the uncomfortable fact that such a departure in public policy would probably be resisted by the East—that is, by the majority—which, of course, would place it entirely beyond the scope of practical politics. In other words, we have an almost exact replica of the present Irish situation—and yet, even that will be solved. While it is true that in our tariff issue, there is no "common ground," there is such a thing as minimum demands and maximum concessions. That is the side of the controversy that must be studied and developed.

The Western farmer suffers under precisely the same disabilities as other large groups of voters. He is just as easily victimized and led astray by the demagogue and rabid partisan politician. In the past, there has been no choice between the great parties on the tariff issue. Hence, he has now thrown them both overboard and has constructed a platform of his own. This is what he officially asks in the way of tariff reform:

1. That the customs duty on goods imported from Great Britain be reduced to one half the rates charged under the general tariff and that further gradual, uniform reductions be made in the remaining tariff on British imports that will ensure

complete free trade between Great Britain and Canada in five years.

2. That the Reciprocity Agreement of 1911, which still remains on the United States' statute books, be accepted by the parliament of Canada.
3. That all food stuff not included in the Reciprocity Agreement be placed on the free list.
4. That agricultural implements, farm machinery, vehicles, fertilizers, coal, lumber, cement, illuminating fuel and lubricating oils be placed on the free list.
5. That the customs tariff on all the necessaries of life be materially reduced.
6. That all tariff concessions granted to other countries be immediately extended to Great Britain.

Let us examine this platform and see what it means in plain English and what it stands for, in the eyes of the average Western farmer. Points 1 and 6 are largely sentimental. All patriotic citizens would hail with satisfaction any such development. Point 2 is of overwhelming importance. Point 3 is desirable, but not absolutely essential. Point 4, he is in deadly earnest about. Point 5 is in the same class as 3. That is the story. In the final analysis we find two planks in the farmers' tariff manifesto, 2 and 4, that will probably represent the minimum demands on the subject on the part of the average, thinking prairie farmer.

These two demands can be met, and should be met, not only because a large section of Canada's producers mean to fight for them, but chiefly because it is essential to our general prosperity that effect should be given to them. I shall be told that in a previous general election Canada, by a large majority, rejected the reciprocity proposals. That is true. But Canada would not do so to-day. No public man, with his ear to the ground, will deny that assertion.

TEN

The Looting of Canada

As has been shown various avenues of protection and aid have been provided for struggling industries in Canada. The levying of import duties prevents the marketing of imported articles in Canada, except at a premium proportionately equal to the amount of protection and theoretically sufficient to permit the home manufacturers of such articles to reap a satisfactory profit. Then there is our much abused bonusing system under which Canada is said to have paid out more money than those fortunate industries have ever paid in wages. But in the financing of most of the large industrial concerns, further protection was accorded, inasmuch as they were permitted to load their capitalization with "water," and thus, in many cases, make twice or three times the profit that the suffering consumer would otherwise have tamely submitted to. It will be observed that there is more than one way of protecting industry.

The method of inflating capital is, of course, familiar to almost everyone. A number of industrial concerns are consolidated into one, and in buying them out fictitious valuations are agreed upon for goodwill, formulae, real estate or leases. Or a new Company is formed to buy out an existing one on the same inflated basis, paying for tangible assets in bonds or preference stock and issuing common stock for goodwill. Or large blocks of common stock are taken by the promoters in payment for services. The general principle is that unless the business makes a success and profits on its common stock, the latter has no special value. This, however, it seldom fails to do, in course of time. The general effect is that while the common stock is almost intrinsically worthless, inasmuch as it represents no realizable asset or even only fictitious assets, the inordinate profits on the actual capital, upon which fixed dividend or interest is paid, soon leave a surplus for the common stock, which begins to rise in value and frequently reaches par. In time accumulated earnings may give it an actual intrinsic value, which has, of course, been entirely contributed by the public.

A protected industry earning six per cent on its actual investment, would cause no particular comment. If, however, the earnings were twelve or eighteen per cent, consumers would demand an explanation. But by the injection of a judicious amount of "water," such a situation is effectually hidden from view, while, quite incidentally, one or two get-rich-quick promoters graduate into the millionaire class. The evil in question is fully recognized and admitted by our public men when out of office. It makes capital campaign talk. With office attained, however, they apparently discover insuperable obstacles to any sort of effective control of the capitalization of industry. In other words our supermen have feet of clay. In this Canada of ours we attempt, and not unsuccessfully, to make our citizens walk the narrow path. The criminal law deals with the thief and the murderer. We even punish the merchant if he cannot substantiate the truth of his advertisements. We fine the careless one for expectorating on the sidewalk or for having weeds growing in his backyard, or chickens running at large. But when we contemplate the proper control of high finance, to prevent millions from being filched from the pockets of Canadian consumers and small investors, we confess that we are up against a veritable stone wall. It simply cannot be done. The stealing of pennies we can punish; the stealing of millions must remain "within the law"! A grateful country even confers titles on the most outstanding exponents of this gentle art.

◆

We have on our statutes a Companies' Act; a formidable document, about the size of a small novel. It contains the most minute directions as to how incorporated companies shall be formed and their business conducted. Woe be unto the transgressor, if only five days notice is given for a meeting where six is clearly prescribed! One step in advance would be a little section calling for a sworn statement from incorporated companies, and those ambitious to become incorporated, showing separately the actual value of all tangible assets under prescribed headings, and the estimated value of intangible assets with supporting evidence as to the value of the estimate, in the form of an auditor's formal certificate. Heavy punishment should also be provided for failing to show this information and for showing it in any misleading way in published statements and prospectuses. This would not completely solve the difficulty, but it would, in many cases, defeat the intentions of swindlers by giving fair notice to the public.

We should also absolutely prohibit the issue of common stock as a bonus to purchasers of bonds or preferred stock. Offers of this sort appear almost daily in the advertizing columns of the press. What justification is there for such pernicious practices? To insist upon all common stock being sold at par and fully paid for would appear to be no more than ordinary honest business. As long as such transactions bear the seal of official authority, it will be impossible to control adequately the capitalization of business and industry. The door is left wide open for dishonest manipulations, over-capitalization and all the other evils from which we are now suffering. If any concern cannot procure its capital by legitimate methods and finds it necessary to resort to shady practises of this character, the country would be better off without it. Special authority to sell stock below par could, if necessary, readily be issued in the case of mining companies and other enterprises of a highly speculative nature, upon proper representations being made by the promoters and after competent investigation by the Government.

It does not seem to be unreasonable for the State to insist upon ordinary honesty in connection with the flotation and management of incorporated companies. The Provincial Governments of Canada have, as a rule, made good progress in this direction, but they only deal with the "small fry." The duty rests upon the Dominion authorities to provide such legislation as will prevent the wholesale "watering" of stock issues. Under the new order of things the public will stand for nothing less. We must have Federal "Blue Sky" legislation and honest financing.

◆

Who are the capitalists? It is customary at farmers' meetings and in the sensational press to refer to capitalists as the "interests." It is the popular conception that the ownership of capital is vested in certain pot-bellied gentlemen whose sole occupation in life is to clip coupons, oppress the poor and corrupt our legislatures. This is scarcely a fair definition.

A glance at the list of shareholders of our railways, banks, and large industrial concerns in Canada hardly confirms any such idea. We find generally that the majority of stockholders are men in very modest circumstances, widows, dependents and a fair sprinkling of well-to-do people. The latter may, and often do, hold the majority of the stock, but not by any means in all cases.

All sorts of drastic proposals were made to "confiscate" wealth. It was a favourite term during the war period. It is well, however, to realise that a very large proportion of the capital invested in Canadian enterprise is composed of the savings of quite plain, ordinary people, who could not, by any stretch of imagination, be included under the general heading of capitalist or "interests."

This is a difficulty that the reformer encounters when he considers the question of squeezing the water out of corporations doing business on inflated capital. Generally these small blocks of shares have been purchased at prevailing market prices and represent *bona fide* investments which cannot be "confiscated" or cancelled with impunity.

The only remedy therefore that can be applied against the recognised evil of "watering" stock issues is to regulate future issues of existing corporations and to exercise eternal vigilance in connection with the formation of new ones. The evil is done and cannot be undone, but the public is entitled to ample protection in the future. The flotation of war loans in Canada has created an enormous number of investors and they will be regarded as the legitimate prey of promoters. They must be amply protected, so far as the State can protect them.

◆

I submit here a statement showing detailed information regarding a number of the larger industrial enterprises of Canada. I have marked opposite each the amount of protection these lusty "infants" enjoy. I have been so anxious to avoid any semblance of unfairness that I have not included in the amount of the protective tariff the extra war-tax of approximately seven per cent. Thus, an industry enjoying 35 per cent protection, was during the later years of the war, and is now, generally on a basis of 42 per cent protection! It is important to bear in mind that I deal with the common stock only. These corporations have, in nearly all cases, bond issues and preferred stock issues in addition to the common stock, amounting to many millions of dollars. I have deducted from their net earnings the amounts required to pay interest on any bond and preferred stock issues. What is shown as earnings in this statement only covers the amount available for distribution amongst the holders of the common stock.

It is also well to remember, as has been pointed out previously, that in most cases, the bulk of the common stock, in some cases practically all of it, merely represents allotments to promoters and bonus allowances to purchasers of the company's preferred stock or bonds. It is therefore in many cases clear loot, upon which the consumer has to provide dividends.

The following table shows earnings of common stock, after deducting dividends on preferred issues, of some industrial enterprises in Canada.

EARNINGS OF COMMON STOCK OF SOME CANADIAN INDUSTRIES

Name of Company	Common Stock outstanding 000's omitted	Average Net Income Applicable to Stock for last 5 years %	Percentage Earned on Stock in last Fiscal Year %	Percentage of same on Market Price of Stock on 1st March, 1919 %	Manufacture	Protection by Customs Tariff
Can. Car and Fdry. Co.	4,963	9.9	17.9	53.0	Steel Axles, etc.	35%
Canada Cement Co.	13,500	5.6	9.6	14.3	Cement	10c. per 100 lbs.
Canadian Cottons, Ltd.	2,715	10.59	18.31	27.0	Cotton Fabrics	25% to 32½%
Canadian General Electric	8,000	11.1	12.4	12.1	Electric Apparatus	27½%
Canadian Locomotive Co.	2,000	15.3	24.1	37.7	Locomotives	35%
Dom. Bridge Co.	6,500	20.7	18.2	14.4	Structural Steel	35%
Dom. Canners, Ltd.	2,794	9.3	19.0	44.2	Canned Fruits	2½c. per lb.
Dom. Steel Co.	37,097	10.9	20.5	33.0	Steel Rails	$7 per ton
Dominion Textile Co.	5,000	13.0	21.9	22.8	Cotton Fabrics	25% to 32½%
Laurentide Co.	9,600	12.2	17.7	9.8	Pulp and Paper	25%
Lake of the Woods Milling Co.	2,100	19.5	33.3	22.2	Wheat Flour	Free
Maple Leaf Milling Co.	2,500	17.4	29.3	23.4	Wheat Flour	Free
Nova Scotia Steel and Coal	15,000	15.1	8.4	12.7	Rolled Bar Iron or Steel	$7 per ton
Ogilvie Flour Mills Co.	2,500	42.9	72.6	38.2	Wheat Flour	Free
Penmans, Ltd.	2,150	22.3	35.3	44.1	Underwear	35%
Price Bros. & Co.	5,000	11.0	18.5	13.2	Pulp	25%
Riordon Pulp & Paper Co.	4,500	10.7	21.4	18.3	Pulp and Paper	25%
Sherwin-Williams Co. of Can.	4,000	8.6	12.8	21.3	Paints	30%
Steel Co. of Canada	11,500	16.1	32.0	44.4	Forgings of Iron or Steel	30%
Woods Manufacturing Co., Ltd.	1,718	13.4	25.2	30.0	Jute Bags, etc.	20%

ELEVEN

Scientific and Commercial Research

CANADA HAS IN HER public services at Ottawa, all the human material necessary to promote a vigorous development policy. But it is scattered, ineffectively organized and in many instances, thoroughly discouraged and demoralised. We have first an "Honorary Advisory Council for Scientific and Industrial Research." The very name would damn it forever. This body undertakes industrial investigation and is building up a technical staff. Its administration is at present under the control of a most able and highly qualified chairman. Then we have the "Conservation Commission," also undertaking somewhat similar work and also surrounded with a technical staff. We have the Dominion Department of Mines conducting investigation within its own field, which, of course, pretty nearly covers everything there is to be done. That also has a large and highly qualified staff. In addition to this, in the Province of British Columbia, and in each of the Eastern Provinces, a Mining Department is maintained. In the Department of Forestry, the Conservation Commission is very active and is well equipped for useful work. The Department of the Interior, however, administers Canada's forests, except where natural resources are under Provincial Control, in which cases local departments are maintained. This department also promotes tree planting in Western Canada most efficiently. Our fisheries are very ably looked after by one Department in Ottawa, with occasional duplication by the Conservation Commission. Each one of these Departments and Branches publishes in blue books or in pamphlets, formidable reports on its technical work and investigation, which, of course, are hardly ever read by anyone. If one wanted everything that had been published to date on any given subject, he would probably have to get into communication with three or more different sources. There is absolutely no general clearing house for technical information, and there is a vast amount of useful information going to waste, simply because there is no effort made to co-ordinate it for useful purposes.

These are some of the conditions that handicapped the Allies in the early stages of the Great War. Unless Canada's future industrial expansion is to be endangered we must enlist the services of our outstanding men; we must no longer waste official energy, or any other good material available, for which the country pays.

Great Britain's known coal deposits amount to 189 billion tons. Canada possesses twelve hundred billion tons of coal, which means three quarters of all the coal deposits in the whole of the British Empire, and one twelfth of the known coal deposits of the world. These deposits are not by any means inaccessible. They are in fact in almost all cases located near railway lines, and, in some instances, on tidewater. During 1917 we used in Canada nearly 35 million tons of coal. And we mined in Canada 14 million tons, out of which we exported 1¾ million tons. We imported from the United States 22½ million tons or approximately two-thirds of all the coal we used! This looks queer. I mention it only to impress upon the reader the fact that to make laborious analyses of our coal does not solve our problem, which is entirely one of markets for our products. It is primarily commercial investigation and exploitation Canada needs, with such technical and scientific assistance as each problem may call for.

◆

I realize that it is rank heresy to criticize the work of scientific men. But I am not going to criticize their scientific work. I am going to confine my remarks to the business aspect of the case. A business Government would call a joint meeting of all those now engaged on technical research work and ask for report and suggestions. Fur-

ther, let some specially qualified business man be appointed to in-
vestigate the scope of each department or branch affected; let him
report his finding to a select committee of the Privy Council, and so
co-operate in bringing order out of the present chaos by the creation of some central supreme body or by constituting one of the existing organizations, such as the Honorary Advisory Council, the
central clearing house with the necessary authority to discontinue
aimless scientific investigation and to focus the effort of Canada's
scientific staffs upon practical and useful objectives. Such method,
organized along rational lines to get results, would co-ordinate existing effort, abolish duplication and inform the public.

While on this subject, it is appropriate to offer a few remarks
touching a very common fallacy entertained by Governments,
namely, that technically-qualified men are able to advise intelligently on matters of pure business. They have their proper field
and so has the business man. There should be the clearest distinction made, however. On such a board as referred to above, the clear
headed business executive should find a prominent place. Immediately on organization, it would compile a list of the most highly
qualified technical experts in Canada in private employ. It would
then circularise these men, stating the objects of the organization
and inviting their patriotic co-operation. This would doubtless be
enthusiastically and spontaneously forthcoming. It should be
realised that however skilled may be the technical men employed
permanently by the Government or engaged in research work in
connection with our various universities, they cannot possibly hope
to speak authoritatively on every subject and every phase of
scientific research. Besides, they are too far removed from the field
where practical results only will count, and where new avenues of
investigation are daily opening up. Consequently, they do not always know the last word on any subject. It would, therefore, naturally suggest itself to a business man that instead of maintaining
large expensive technical staffs at headquarters, it would be much
more economical, and certainly much more effective, to arrange
temporarily to utilize specialist talent in connection with specific
lines of investigation.

But it is not alone in the field of scientific research that new ground should be broken. Good work could be done through governmental channels in a dozen other directions. We need some trade body with proper machinery, to give the helping hand in the marketing of our products and in the discovery of new markets.

Our statistical system, as far as it deals with interprovincial trade, could with advantage be greatly augmented. The volume and value of internal trade are unknown factors in Canada. In connection with our export trade, we have much to learn from our recent foe in Europe. Germany's system of commercial intelligence and financial accommodation gave results which it would be worth our while to study. The development of our municipal markets is another subject worthy of consideration. Much has been done in Europe in this direction, and the example might well be followed in Canada. This would tend to bring the smaller producers and consumers closer together, with the elimination of distribution cost. Standardization of products, particularly for the export markets, would bear fruit, and promote Canadian industry. All these tasks require leadership, which can best be furnished by the Government.

TWELVE

A National Trial Balance

IT WILL BE INSTRUCTIVE to make a brief survey of the financial standing, and past financial record, of this enterprise called the Dominion of Canada. I shall deal with the head office first. The sub-offices, called the Provinces, and the country branches, called the Municipalities, will also be lightly touched upon.

Canada started business in 1867 with a gross debt of 93 million dollars and an interest liability of 4½ millions. I shall not deduct the assets, as outside the sinking fund, they are not in liquid form and are not realizable. No one wants to buy a Post Office or a bridge, even if we were able to sell it. At that period Canada's total income from taxation was about 11½ million dollars. I deal in round numbers, as too much detail is confusing and quite unnecessary for our purpose. Twenty years after, our debt had increased to 273 millions, interest liability 9½ millions, and revenue 28½ millions. In 1908, forty-one years after Confederation, our debt was 408 million dollars, interest liability 11 millions, and our taxation revenue 73⅓ millions. In 1914 the war broke out. Our debt increased to 544⅓ millions, interest engagements 12¾ millions and revenue from taxes 127½ millions. We ended the war with approximately 1,200 millions of gross public debt, interest engagements of about 26 millions per annum, and annual revenue from taxation of somewhere near 176 million dollars. Our reconstruction programme will doubtless lead to increased liability.

Dealing now more particularly with the question of public debt, it is interesting to take a glimpse of the position of the various provinces in this respect up to the end of their last fiscal years:

Prince Edward Island	$11,154,000
Nova Scotia	13,910,000
New Brunswick	17,827,000
Quebec	38,449,000
Ontario	61,795,000
Manitoba	38,506,000
Saskatchewan	26,797,000
Alberta	30,595,000
British Columbia	35,673,000
Total	$264,706,000

These figures are not absolutely correct. I defy the most expert auditor to dig out the exact figures. Each province has a beautiful system of accounts of its own, generally designed to hide the facts and confuse the public.

But when we enter the field of municipal indebtedness, we behold chaos in its most typical form. It should be some concern of Canada, and Canada's creditors, to know the total liabilities of our municipalities. There is, however, no individual in the whole, wide world who knows that. If a business concern kept track of its gross liabilities in this way, the courts would be called upon to interfere. However, I am going to make a guess based on certain known factors. We have records available from 62 cities and towns in Canada, showing the total indebtedness to be 456 million dollars. The total population of these centres is, I find, 2,598,000. This makes the indebtedness per head $210.17. As these cities and towns are so located as to be fairly representative of the whole, we shall not be very far wrong in applying the latter figure as the key to the whole situation. Therefore, the total population in Canada residing in urban communities of over 500 inhabitants being 3,281,000, the total municipal indebtedness of Canada, based on $210.17 per head, would be 689½ million dollars. It will be noticed, that this amount comes next in importance to our present Federal indebtedness, and, outside our obligations due strictly to unforeseen expenditure for purposes of war, is the most considerable item in Canada's total liability.

To sum up, we find our public indebtedness, half of which is probably held internally, distributed as follows:

Head Office	1,200 millions
Sub Offices	264½ millions
Country Branches	689½ millions
Total	2,154 millions

What does that mean? We have in Canada 1½ million families. Each family is apparently responsible for the sum of $1,436 of public liabilities in addition to its private liabilities, including the mortgage on the old homestead. Of course, the sheriff is not coming in tomorrow to collect this amount under distress warrant, the creditors being kind, good people who will wait—as long as you pay your interest fairly promptly. But with the stress of the reconstruction period ahead, it will do no harm, when you make up your list of liabilities, to add the sum of $1,436 just to get used to the idea that you must pay interest on this with the same regularity as you pay your life insurance premium or the instalments on your cheerful little home. This is the first lesson that the New Canada has to learn.

In discussing the liabilities of Canada, we have hitherto dealt exclusively with public liabilities, that is, those owed by the State, including the provinces and municipalities, which must be carried and repaid by taxation. These are partly owed to our own citizens and partly to residents and institutions in other countries.

It is of interest in this connection to give a bird's eye view of Canada's external liabilities, public and private. Fred. M. Field and the "Monetary Times" give the following information on the subject:

British Capital Invested in Canada

20 Branch Plants, average capital, $300,000	$6,000,000
Canadian Bank Shares held by Industrial Purchasers	2,000,000
Investments with Loan & Mortgage Companies	12,000,000
British Insurance Companies' Assets in Canada	30,000,000
Municipals sold Privately	15,000,000
Industrial Investments	29,000,000
Mining Investments	59,000,000
Land and Timber Purchases	40,000,000
Town and City Purchases	25,000,000
Canadian Flotations, 1905–1913	1,660,900,000
Total	$1,878,900,000

United States Capital Invested in Canada

500 Branch Firms (average investment $300,000)	$150,000,000
Government, Municipal and Corporation Bonds (1905–1913)	123,743,000
Government, Municipal and Corporation Bonds (1914–1917)	590,506,000
Insurance Company Investments	94,276,000
British Columbia Mills and Timber	75,000,000
British Columbia Mines	62,000,000
British Columbia Land Transactions	60,000,000
Prairie Province Land Transactions	41,000,000
City and Town Properties	20,000,000
Maritime Province Investments	13,125,000
Industrial Investments (Miscellaneous)	12,200,000
Prairie Province Timber and Mines	10,500,000
Agricultural Implement Firms	9,250,000
Packing Plants	6,750,000
Theatrical Enterprises	3,500,000
Prince Edward Island (Fox Farms)	1,000,000
Total	$1,272,850,000

The British figures here quoted do not go beyond 1913. It is, however, estimated that Canadian flotations in London up to 1918 have amounted to $937,864,000. This would make a total of $2,816,764,000. Adding this amount to our liabilities to the United States, we find Canada's total estimated external capital liability to be about 4,089 million dollars, as far as these two countries are concerned. Other countries have investments in Canada, notably France and Holland. If we estimate our total capital liabilities at somewhere below five billions, we shall probably not be far wrong. This is not, of course, a floating liability. It is invested capital upon which, however, we are expected to pay either interest or dividends.

Those who are enthusiastic about public ownership should study these figures. There is ample food for reflection. Our foreign obligations are sacred and cannot be discharged by a wave of the hand and, above all, if there is any doubt as to the security, this capital takes wings as speedily as possible, and the flow of new capital stops. Our prosperity, therefore, depends largely upon our ability to secure capital absolutely against experimental and predatory legislation. Some of our western provincial governments apparently do not clearly realize that fact.

In addition to our capital obligations, we have certain external floating liabilities varying, of course, from day to day. First of all, we have the accrued interest and dividends on capital investments. On an average basis of three per cent, they would amount to 150 million dollars. The balance, that is, of our commercial liabilities to other countries in excess of what they owe us, is difficult to get at. The average trade balance against us does not tell the story for various reasons. When we add these items to our capital liabilities, we shall probably find that Canada's total external debt will not exceed by any considerable amount the sum of five billion dollars.

◆

Having examined the debit side of Canada's ledger, it will be interesting also to look into the value of those things which constitute the credit. From this, of course, must be deducted our estimated external liability due to borrowings by private or corporate enterprise, which is estimated at 2½ billion dollars and probably one billion of public liability. The balance will be our net worth as a nation. The following is the estimated gross national wealth of Canada:

Items	Estimated present value
Agriculture—Improved lands	$2,792,229,000
Buildings	927,548,000
Implements	387,079,000
Live stock	1,102,261,000
Fishing—Total capital invested	47,143,125
Mines—Value of buildings and plant	140,000,000
Manufactures—Plant and working capital	2,000,000,000
Railways	2,000,000,000
Street railways	160,000,000
Canals	123,000,000
Shipping	35,000,000
Telegraphs	10,000,000
Telephones	95,000,000
Real estate and buildings in cities and towns based on assessments of 140 localities	3,500,000,000
Clothing, furniture and personal effects	800,000,000
Coin and bullion—Held by Receiver General	119,000,000
Specie in banks	82,000,000
Value of token currency	7,500,000
Imported merchandise in store	250,000,000
Current production—Agriculture	1,621,028,000
Fishing	39,000,000
Forestry	175,000,000
Mining	190,000,000
Manufacturing	2,400,000,000
Total	$19,002,788,125

It is estimated that with this investment Canada earned in the way of salaries and wages about 881 million dollars in 1911, which, with advances that have since taken place, would bring the amount up to 1,000 millions for the year 1919, and it is estimated that the income available for living of those who are in business for themselves, or practising professions, will approach 1,200 millions, making a total national income of approximately 2,200 millions per annum under present economic conditions. This is an average of about $259 per annum for every man, woman and child in Canada or $1,295 for an average family unit of five.

It is now in order to devote a few remarks to the question of running expenses and resources. Our expenditure per head for Federal administration, interest on debt, etc., for the year 1870 was $4.48, and our revenue per head was $5.55. Those were the days of the simple life. We had 3½ million people to care for who were largely devoting their attention to agriculture and gave little trouble. In 1910 we had doubled our population almost exactly, but our "overhead" was beginning to run away with us. Our expenditure per head had jumped to $11.48 and the patient taxpayer was contributing $14.67 per head of population. That year there was evidently something left over to reduce our public debt. Then the war came along and the figure immediately began to soar uncomfortably. In 1917 the expenditure per head was $17.77 and the revenue $27.82. We had an estimated population of 8⅓ million people.

Now what about the future? I am not going to confuse the reader with spectacular references to "consolidated fund," "sinking fund" or any of the other hocus-pocus of the counting house. We know that it will cost us at least 300 million dollars a year to run Federal Canada, pay interest on debt, look after pensions and pay current expenses not chargeable against capital account. It may, and probably will, cost us considerably more. This minimum would involve an average annual contribution per head of population of about $37. Of course, in addition to this, the Provinces and municipalities will call upon us to put up at least a similar amount. It would not be so bad if we husky males did not have to pay for the ladies, the babies, the minors and the unattached male drifters. If each man pays for five persons, which is approximately what our taxpayer will have to do, his Federal tax will amount to $185 per head and his total tax—Federal, Provincial and Municipal—to approximately

$370 per annum. This is somewhat of a load. The gross per capita income is estimated at $259 per annum for the entire population, men, women and children and the taxation rate for all purposes at $74 per annum. Our average family unit has a revenue of $1,295 and will pay $370 in taxes, or approximately 30 per cent. This, of course, includes consumption taxation. It will certainly cut into our income!

———————◆———————

It is interesting to compare these figures with the financial situation in Great Britain, so as to form a better conception of the relative magnitude of Canada's financial problem. Prior to the war, the total wealth of the United Kingdom was about 80 billion dollars and the national income 10 billion dollars. It is estimated that by this time the British National Debt amounts to 40 per cent of the total estimated wealth of that country. Canada's Federal debt is less than eight per cent of her developed resources. Decidedly, our post-war financial problem looks very insignificant in comparison. In Great Britain it is expected that the normal taxation will reach 755 million pounds per annum, being at the rate of about $105 per capita, compared with our per capita requirements per annum for Federal purposes only of $37!

It is at once conceded that this is not time for self-satisfied national indolence and foolish optimism. But the worst enemy of Canada today is the brooding pessimist—the blue-ruin prophet—that intolerable drag on national progress. Compare the conditions in this splendid young country of ours with those in war-torn, war-weary Europe. Realise that in those older civilizations almost every natural resource has been developed and exploited for centuries at high pressure. The soils have lost their virgin fertility and are coaxed to produce crops only by intensive culture and artificial fertilization and at great cost. Every available corner of these older countries has for ages done its part in agricultural production. There are no new coal or mineral resources to be discovered and exploited. The creation of new wealth is limited by the possibility of making the human machine more efficient than it was before. And they cannot even add materially to the number of human working units.

Now, Mr. Pessimist, look at Canada. Do you know how to look at Canada with the knowing, appraising, intelligent eye? If you do, are you not amazed at her enormous, potential, natural wealth? The surface of her wonderful agricultural empire has scarcely been scratched and yet she is feeding millions. Her undeveloped coal, oil, power, forest and mineral resources defy the wildest flights of imagination. The wealth of the Indies fades into insignificance in comparison. Canada's forests and fisheries alone could make a nation prosperous. But, above all, there are the great advantages of her invigorating, healthy climate and clean environments and their priceless product—the virile man and woman.

Canada is an empire of boundless opportunities. We owe now a matter of a billion dollars or so, on account of the war, which we figure out at so much per head of population. Very well. We can double our population and cut the debt in two. We can treble the population and have it reduced to a mere insignificant amount. Our safety lies in the outstanding fact that we can multiply our present population by ten and still have ample elbow room and call aloud for more men and women to come to our shores to help us develop our resources and, incidentally, make happy and prosperous homes for themselves!

Wake up, Industrial Canada! This is the day for the heroic attitude of mind. Are you in doubt as to the wisdom of going full speed ahead—are you tempted to "play safe"? Did the boys in the front trenches "play safe"? If they had done so, where would you and your precious industry be today? Were they pessimistic and downhearted during the darkest days of the war? Mr. Industrialist, you have nothing but sordid, material things to lose, and it is your turn to act. Hitch your waggon to a star! Discard your cold, calculating caution and dispel the gloom of panic. Our nation is in the making at this hour and this is the time for great decisions. See that yours is dictated by a sense of public duty and patriotism and not solely influenced by cowardly, timid motives. If you meet the future with that degree of confidence and assurance which the whole situation amply warrants, all will be well.

I want to urge upon all classes in Canada at this moment to have done with pessimism, and to take up cheerfully our comparatively easy burden with unbounded confidence in our ability to discharge our obligations in full. Those who, in this vital period of the world's history, are privileged to live in this virgin land of ours may regard themselves as fortunate in comparison with others who must solve laboriously the infinitely harder problems facing the inhabitant of European countries, surrounded by all the limitations of older civilizations. They have for many centuries drawn heavily against nature's ever-diminishing savings account, while we, in Canada, have in that bank a balance to our credit, the extent of which defies human calculation.

THIRTEEN

Raising the Wind

IN THE AFFAIRS OF the nations concerned the Treasury Departments of the Governments of Great Britain and the United States loom up much more prominently than Canada's Finance Department. This, no doubt, is partly due to the fact that the financial problem of this country has never been acute. But it is becoming so now. And the time has clearly arrived when our Federal Finance Department, and our Finance Minister, must take the same dominant place as in other countries. We do recognize, in an unofficial sort of way that the portfolio of Finance comes next in importance to the Prime Minister, but this vague notion should be translated into an actuality. In all seriousness, the "water tight" department scheme at Ottawa must go, and those who obstruct the removal of the administrative bulkheads should go with them. We have reached a crisis in the history of our country when the closest team work becomes an absolute essential to the introduction of business methods in our administration. The Prime Minister is, of course, supposed to be the connecting link between departments, but he now moves in a sphere far removed from mere departmental adjustments. Council is a poor medium for promoting team work on the part of its individual members. Authorized leadership and cabinet discipline are what we require just now. The remedy is to clothe the Finance Minister with wide powers, second only to those of the Prime Minister, or rather to delegate some of the powers of the latter to the Finance Minister. He should be in a position to remonstrate with, and to dictate policy to, his colleagues, without apology.

I know precisely the sort of Finance Minister Canada really requires in the present crisis. He should possess the capacity of the present Prime Minister for sane, judicial reflection, Mr. Rowell's high sense of public duty, and the analytical, rapierlike mind of Sir George Foster, coupled with his parsimonious inclinations. With the inscrutable face and the courageous, contemptuous disregard for public opinion of Mr. Sifton, he should have the broad vision of Sir Thomas White and the untiring industry of Mr. Calder. This composite super-Finance Minister would, of course, be more monster than human. He would be blind to everything except public interest. He would separate you from your last crust with a shrug of his shoulder. Our fiscal machine would be as efficient as the juggernaut, and so cordially hated that the people would proceed to smash it. All of which goes to show that democracy hates efficiency.

Until this weird creature of the imagination turns up and offers his services for a dollar a year, Canada may consider herself singularly fortunate in the present incumbent of this important post. He was not a prominent figure on the political horizon even a few years ago. Consequently, he is not steeped in unwholesome party politics. We may expect from him more than a partisan consideration of national problems. Sir Thomas White is a broad-gauge, patriotic man, not unwise politically, very approachable and tolerant in his views. There is perhaps no better human material in sight in our public life for the important responsibilities of "raising the wind" in order that we may escape the whirlwind.

———————————◆———————————

Decidedly, the most important information the Government of Canada needs today is just how to obtain the necessary revenue without detrimental effects on the development of our country.

Our Federal Finance Department should employ constantly several highly paid men, trained in various lines of activity, to conduct a painstaking, detailed investigation into every possible source of revenue the Government might fairly and safely utilize, to discover feasible sources of taxation and to work out all the details for incorporation in the budget. By studying the British fiscal proposals, it will be found that we have in Canada various sources of revenue that have not yet been tapped. There are great possibilities in the direction of luxury taxation. Those who, in a crisis like the present, desire to indulge in high living, should pay for the privilege.

For goodness sake, let us endeavour to get out of the rut of brainless imitativeness and see if we cannot be original, be ourselves, for a change. Tamely copying fiscal policies of other countries is such a tiresome confession of stupid incapacity. I cannot recall, at this moment, any important plan of an original character, in the way of war administration, that we worked out in Canada during the past strenuous years, except our system of pensions and of vocational training of disabled soldiers, which is a model of efficiency. Everything else was copied from other countries and generally a couple of years late in being put into force. Do let us wake up and become impressed with the idea that we, in Canada, have our own peculiar handicaps to overcome in our own peculiar way.

◆

There are many dangers assailing democracy on every side. One of the greatest is the demagogue in responsible places. His stock in trade is destructive criticism. He plays on the ignorance of the multitude. The only safeguard against this menace is enlightened public opinion. Our public life is honeycombed with this class of politician, who frequently drives Governments into unwise and unfair legislation, simply as a concession to popular clamour, based on shallow, opportunist argument.

We have seen a beautiful example of this poisonous propaganda in connection with the imposition of business taxation in Canada. The Business Profits War Tax Act, as now amended, provides that in the case of all businesses having a capital of $50,000 and over, the Government collects 25 per cent of the net profits over 7 per cent and not exceeding 15 per cent; 50 per cent of the profits over 15 per cent and not exceeding 20 per cent; and 75 per cent of the profits beyond 20 per cent. In all cases where a business has a capital of $25,000 and under $50,000, the Government takes 25 per cent of all profits in excess of 10 per cent on the capital employed. Concerns employing capital of less than $25,000 are exempted, with the exception of those dealing in munitions or war supplies. As might be expected, this legislation proved exceedingly popular amongst the masses. It was regarded as a thoroughly "democratic" measure. The man on the street did not pause to reason the thing out. It looked well on the face of it and he was amply satisfied. It was a clear case of "corporation baiting."

If we expect Canadian industry and business to prosper and expand, we must remove obstacles rather than impose them.

To say to an industry: "You made a profit of $20,000 last year on a capital of $60,000. Therefore, you can afford to pay in cash to the Government the sum of so many thousand dollars," is utterly absurd. Who knows what the financial requirements and engagements of this particular industry are? What are the pressing floating liabilities that must be paid out of earnings? What are the future chances of heavy losses on operations against which cash reserves must be built up to enable the concern to carry on? Or what the necessity for providing a fund to take up past losses? What amount of cash is urgently needed to replace worn-out equipment or to install modern equipment to reduce cost of production? One can quite imagine that an industry might appear to be making large earnings, but might easily be absolutely crippled by the withdrawal of the amount of cash involved under the present taxation system.

The business tax is not, in the least, democratic. It is simply destructive. In our fiscal policy the broad principle should be laid down that no citizen shall escape his just tax.

Business earnings should not be subject to taxation until they are available for distribution in cash, when the proper tax should promptly be deducted and remitted direct to the Government and the balance only paid over to the shareholder.

◆

I read some time ago in a Toronto weekly a most amusing biographical sketch of our famous Fathers of Confederation. All my illusions were cruelly shattered. They were pictured as a most mediocre set of men, many of them greatly addicted to the unwise use of alcoholic stimulants, and some with subsequent records that drove them from public life. Upon looking over the taxation provisions of the British North America Act, I am forced to the conclusion that this humourist did not wander far from the truth.

In some Provinces, the individual pays three separate taxes on income—to the Federal and Provincial Governments as well as to the municipality in which he resides. There seems to be neither reason nor method in our whole taxation scheme in Canada, and some quick and effective work in the way of constitutional amendments would seem to be urgently necessary. Certainly, taxation on income, which is bound to become the main source of revenue for the Federal Government, must be reserved absolutely for the Dominion. There can be no question that intelligent legislation cannot be proposed on this subject unless the Government enjoys a monopoly on this tax. After a fair income tax plan has been worked out by the Federal Government, and received the sanction of Parliament, there is at present no assurance whatever that a Province or municipality may not step in and levy additional taxes on income that will upset the whole equilibrium of the scheme.

It is also reasonably clear that inheritance taxation should be reserved exclusively for the Dominion. To create a sinking fund for the repayment of our public debt, the rational system would seem to be to impose a scientifically graduated Federal inheritance tax, designed so as in time to take up most of the principal liability, and to use other means of taxation for the liquidation of interest, and for the consolidated fund expenditure.

It is realized that such a method is open to some objections, the principal one being that most estates upon which a drastic inheritance tax would be levied could not pay a large proportion of cash. Provision could, however, readily be made for the State to take over stocks, bonds and other investments at their proper valuation, so as not to impede the progress of industry generally, or to place any undue burden on an estate liable to heavy taxation. Shares in industrial enterprises forming part of such estates could readily be taken over by the Government and the income collected for the benefit of the people of Canada. The Public Trustee in England administers thousands of estates there and the precedent was set in Canada when we provided an organization to deal with the administration of alien enemy property. Even if an inheritance tax on the basis of the one imposed in Great Britain was adopted, it would yield a very considerable revenue, which would increase with population and the prosperity of the country.

Entirely apart from the question of revenue, a heavy inheritance tax is in line with advanced thought. It distinctly makes for a more even distribution of wealth amongst the people. While the State, as at present constituted, may not materially interfere with the business activities of its individual citizen during his lifetime, it cannot be successfully argued that the handing down of huge estates from father to son is in the interest of the latter or in the public interest. In fact, it is entirely contrary to public interest. Civilized society cannot accept the principle that the individual born into the lap of luxury is entitled to everything life can give, without individual effort. The mere accident of birth should not be the governing factor. Every citizen in the model democracy should be usefully employed as long as he is able to work, and should have no right to more than a modest portion of any estate left by bequest. The balance should be appropriated for public purposes, after taking suitable care of minors, and female or aged dependents.

The late Colonel Roosevelt and many illustrious statesmen have been firm and consistent believers in drastic inheritance taxation, not alone as a means of producing revenue for the State, but also to correct social inequalities. It is scarcely open to doubt that boys who are compelled to make their own way in life, after having obtained a reasonably good education, make better citizens in the end than those who, provided for through the thrift and exertion of others, frequently fall a victim to idle and vicious habits. It is quite proper and in the public interest that the State should have some jurisdiction over the wealth of deceased citizens.

◆

There cannot be any question that whatever amount of revenue the Government is able to collect by way of taxation on imports can be collected with equal certainty by direct taxation, or through any other channel, but probably not with equal facility from the identical man who paid it before. There is the rub.

The following seems to be the case, as far as I can size it up:

1. A direct tax involves positive knowledge on the part of each taxpayer of the exact amount of his contribution. Intelligent exemptions can, therefore, be made.

2. An indirect tax shrouds the whole transaction in mystery. No one knows what he pays. No intelligent exemption can, therefore, be made. The system is, consequently, unsound and unscientific and should be avoided as far as possible.

3. Collecting the bulk of Canada's necessary revenue by means of direct taxation, therefore, resolves itself into a complete revision of the present scale of income taxation, including a lower exemption; all of which creates a most uncomfortable political problem.

There is no use denying that this political problem is a real one and even a serious one. But those who discuss the proposal as beyond the scope of practical politics surely admit tacitly that under present conditions the less affluent classes may be bearing an unduly heavy proportion of the burden of indirect taxation, without knowing it. Consumption taxes on luxuries can still be maintained, also on certain necessities as in the British plan, but the income, being the fairest basis of taxation, should assuredly be made the corner-stone of our taxation policy rather than merely incidental to the scheme.

◆

The Great War will be directly responsible for many fundamental changes in our social structure. Even now some of them are taking definite form. One vital effect will unquestionably be that the incidence of taxation all over the world will enlarge its scope. It will graduate from the narrow field of exacting more or less nominal tribute upon the earnings of the citizen for defraying the cost of public services, into the much wider and more important sphere of becoming an effective instrument in promoting a more even distribution of wealth amongst all the citizens of a nation. The doubling and trebling of public revenue requirements to defray the staggering cost of war and its aftermath, will throw on most of the nations of the world, Canada included, a perpetual burden which must of necessity be carried chiefly by those who are best able to bear it, that is, by the rich and the moderately wealthy citizen.

This situation will have a far-reaching effect. It will solve many social problems. Great Britain today takes by direct taxation one-third of the gross annual income of its fairly well-to-do citizen and a very large share of his entire fortune at death. Obviously, in the course of time, great fortunes will automatically disappear. In Canada, with our smaller and less affluent population, the burden may have to be almost equally as great. The State can now perhaps afford largely to shut its eyes to inordinate profits on private enterprise. They must in the end pay tribute and the profiteer will find that he has merely acted as a voluntary taxgatherer for the State. This will presently become an irksome, unpopular and thankless pastime. It may perhaps safely be taken for granted that if the Government of Canada does its duty intelligently, the scheme of taxation will be so adjusted that net earnings on private capital will never be what they were in the past, and thus the levelling process will presently remove the more glaring inequalities that now furnish the favourite text of socialist propaganda.

FOURTEEN

The Farmer and His Taxes

THE FARMER PRESENTS a special problem in taxation owing to the difficulty of ascertaining his net income after making reasonable allowances for all items properly chargeable against business operation. It is putting it mildly to state that the difficulty is further enhanced in Canada owing to the pioneer character of our agriculture and its rough-and-ready business methods.

◆

Speaking by and large, the tariff reform movement is essentially one that comes from the land. The farmers of Canada, constituting fifty-six per cent of the population, have spoken formally on the subject in no uncertain voice. As might be expected, the metropolitan press of our country, while in many instances professing sympathy with the agrarian view, has not been slow in pointing out that revenue is the crux of the situation and that any agitation in favour of a reform that would at once reduce the public revenue by at least fifty per cent, must, in common fairness, be accompanied by some sort of suggestion as to how the financial situation is to be adequately met.

The Canadian farmer has unfortunately failed in this respect to some extent and has apparently been ill-advised and unintelligently led. His class already enjoyed the unenviable reputation of being utterly selfish, narrow and devoid of public spirit. The sarcastic comments in the daily press on his latest venture into the fiscal field have not had a tendency to correct this impression. In fact, it is now firmly rooted in the minds of urban dwellers. The farmers' tariff reform movement is frankly regarded by them as a selfish attempt on the part of the largest class of producers in Canada to shift the burden of taxation from their own shoulders to those of the already overtaxed town and city dwellers. This is an unfortunate, and, I believe, quite erroneous, conception of the situation.

The farmers, as a matter of fact, have steadily and consistently urged the adoption of the Single Tax system in Canada. Under it, there would be no possibility of their escaping taxation. It is only fair that this part of their platform should be considered in conjunction with their tariff reform attitude.

As I have pointed out, the farmer, from a taxgathering point of view, unquestionably presents a problem. What his present contribution is under the import tariff system of collecting revenue no one knows and no one can even estimate. While no definite figures are available on the subject, it is fairly certain that collections under the income tax law now in force, from farmers throughout Canada, will be inconsiderable. Our Finance Department has in all probability regarded the situation as more or less hopeless and has not perhaps even made a very serious study of methods to bring the average farmer successfully within the operation of this tax.

Obviously, it is a most difficult matter to analyze the income and expenditure of the farmer so that a proper basis may be reached for levying income tax. In the first place, only few farmers keep books, or even simple records of their business transactions, and most of them, if asked to fill in forms giving information of the status of their business, would be quite unable to do so. The farmer receives part of his living from his business. The value of this would have to be determined and it is seldom on record. Altogether, it would be an almost impossible task to collect taxes from the farm on an actual income basis.

It seems to me that the single-tax principle might effectively be applied in collecting from the farm the volume of taxation deemed necessary in lieu of income tax. It would be necessary to consider the farmer entirely apart from the regular operation of the income tax and then adjust the import tariff accordingly. Having estimated the additional amount to be collected from Canadian farms, simply make a levy on all agricultural lands in Canada of so much per acre.

◆

In working out a land tax system applicable to agriculture in Canada, exemption provisions would have to be carefully drafted. A reasonable exemption period would need to be given new settlers before the Act became operative in their cases. The possibility of extended crop failure would have to be contemplated and provided for by conferring power on the Governor-in-Council to postpone the collection of land taxes within any area so affected. Above all, the character of lands embraced in farms would need to be classified roughly, at least, if full justice were to be done to each holder. It is obvious that stony or swampy areas could not fairly be taxed on the same basis as lands capable of yielding expensive and remunerative crops. The tax would probably also have to be graduated according to average land value in each province, and possibly with reference to distance from railway transportation and markets.

FIFTEEN

Rural Credit

WE HAVE BEEN TOLD by our leading financial men that our banking system is the best in the world. It probably is—for the banks. It may be also for industry and commerce. That it was specially designed to meet the requirements of the latter is clear. From the point of view of agriculture, it leaves much to be desired.

Our whole system of enormously large financial corporations, with branches scattered all over Canada, does not lend itself successfully to business with the farmer, for the simple reason that the banking risk involved in agricultural loans cannot be estimated on the basis that applies in connection with commercial loans. Once a farmer has made his start and purchased his plant, he has invested his entire capital in fixed assets and in some cases has considerable liabilities attached to them. Individual loaning in such a case would be considered reckless banking. The farmer with sufficient liquid assets to command a loan is precisely the farmer who probably does not need it. The real assets of the average farmer, compelled to use the bank, are of course, the fixed and moral assets—the fact that he has a large equity in his land, even though it may be mortgaged, that he has a wife and children and has taken root in his own soil, that he has lived in the district for years and bears a good character. These assets, however, are seldom considered by the average chartered bank, and from a business point of view, one cannot criticize. It is the system that falls short.

The business of the chartered bank is to lend against unpledged liquid assets, taking security in certain cases. Useful amendments have been made to the Act in recent years to enable banks to lend to farmers against definite security. The exemption provisions, however, make farm loans a hazardous risk. I am inclined to think that the various Provincial Governments might in conference with delegates from agricultural organizations, advantageously reconsider the exemptions granted farmers. Altogether, this class of business cannot be satisfactorily handled through the present organization of our banks and the machinery now available. The very practice of sending quite young men out as managers of branches in rural districts and after a brief interval transferring them elsewhere by way of promotion, is not calculated to bring the farmer and his bank representative into very intimate relations. They hardly get to know each other before a new manager arrives and the process of establishing confidential contact has to be begun all over again. Besides, these young men have little authority except in regard to trifling loans and are continually under the iron rod of the head office.

---◆---

Numerous British Royal Commissions have visited Denmark during recent years to study the system and method of financial cooperation so successfully practised there. I have in mind one Commission that condemned the whole Danish system unstintingly, on the ground that the average debt of the farmer there was the greatest per capita of any agricultural country in Europe, or probably in the world. This argument, however, was successfully refuted by a leading economist, who pointed out that the facility with which the Danish farmer could command capital, both short term and long term, at a low rate of interest, was precisely the fundamental reason for the unprecedented agricultural prosperity of that country.

The widest possible credit, at the lowest rate of interest, is an essential in agricultural development. Where these conditions prevail, agriculture prospers.

We are exceedingly short of live stock in Canada. There are many causes assigned for this situation, which appears somewhat paradoxical to the man from the city or town, who has not lived close to the soil. He attributes it to a studied neglect on the part of the farmer in respect of one branch of his business, which infallibly would lead to unqualified success if once he could be persuaded to try it. This, of course, may be at once dismissed as an absolutely absurd proposition.

It is altogether a question of capital. The farmer must purchase foundation stock, provide certain buildings, grow additional fodder crops, etc. How are we going to solve it? Not by any sort of educational propaganda, technical or commercial. That live stock on the farm is a desirable proposition, no one disputes. It is self-evident. If there is any immediate solution in sight it lies in the extension of rural credit.

My criticism is exclusively confined to the absence in Canada of a banking organization specially designed to meeting agricultural requirements in a new country.

Another difficulty is that present bank advances are of too temporary a nature. Our banks are great sticklers for "liquid" assets. A farm loan may be made for three months and renewed on maturity. But difficulties are raised by the Head Office when renewals are too frequently requested. The policy is that the bank must be repaid, at least, within the year. The whole transaction is a temporary one, which is not what the farmer wants. He cannot profitably invest in live stock knowing that he has to realize within a year. It is not worth while for a farmer to borrow on such conditions for live stock investment. The attitude of the chartered bank is that it cannot undertake to supply permanent capital to its customers. Its mission is to supplement temporarily their working capital. As regards industry and commerce, that is quite an unassailable position. The farmer, however, can be only partly benefitted by such a limited measure of financial assistance.

───────────◆───────────

In the United States the country's financial business is based on local "State" and "National" banks. The owner of the small bank most frequently manages the business. He is generally a leading man in the community and knows every farmer in the district personally. Two or more such banks, frequently with a capital as low as $50,000, compete for business in most rural centres. With the recent establishment of great regional banks, every facility now exists for rediscounting of farmers' paper, so that a large loaning business can actually be done on comparatively small capital. The moral asset is, of course, the keystone of loaning to farmers by these institutions, and the interest rate is generally high, although seldom higher than in our West. The system is well adapted for the requirements of a new agricultural country, but I think Canada might evolve something better; possibly on the co-operative plan.

The Government of the United States has, however, within the past few years, given very considerable attention to the question of providing machinery for extended loans to farmers on real estate security at low rates of interest. After a very searching investigation into the rural credit systems of various countries throughout the world, legislation was brought in, under which a Federal Farm Loan Bureau was established to arrange long term credits. The Federal Farm Loan Act will enable farmers throughout the United States to borrow any sum from $100 up to $10,000 at from five to forty year periods. The basis adopted in fixing rates is to advance up to 50 per cent of the land value and up to 20 per cent of the value of the permanent, insured improvements on the land.

———————◆———————

In the Dominion of New Zealand the problem seems to have been satisfactorily solved. After a complete investigation of European agricultural credit-systems by a commission, that colony came to the conclusion that a plan to furnish cheap money to farmers came well within the scope of practical politics. It was realized there that no private concern or corporation could loan money to farmers for a sufficiently long period, and at a sufficiently low rate of interest, to enable him to meet his interest and principal payments from the earnings of the farm and, at the same time, to take care of his living expenses and necessary improvements. It was felt that the repayment of loans to private enterprise would often be made by farmers at a sacrifice. The people of New Zealand thought that it was most desirable to enable their rural population to surround themselves with comforts and conveniences that would make life on the land specially attractive, all of which required moderate capital. In 1894, legislation was passed by the Parliament of New Zealand, entitled "Advances to Settlers Act." Capital was raised in Europe on Government guaranteed bonds and loaned to farmers through a chain of "Advances to Settlers Offices." This organization was contemplated under the Act. In 20 years, over seventy million dollars was loaned on this basis, the rate of interest being 1% over the actual cost of the money to the Government, which was to cover working expenses and flotation charges, also to create a reserve fund. Nearly two million dollars now stands to the credit of this fund. The system is not on a co-operative basis inasmuch as each borrower is only responsible for his own liability. The 1% feature, however, provides against losses. So far there have only been 35 foreclosures under this Act; no losses whatever have been sustained, and the actual cost of the administration has been reasonable.

It is interesting to study the result of this rural credit system. When it went into effect the per capita value of domestic products exported annually from New Zealand amounted to approximately $30, while in 1912 they had risen to $111.78, which was then supposed to be the highest of any country in the world. The number of savings-accounts and amount to their credit are also reputed to be the largest in the world in proportion to population. The whole agricultural situation in New Zealand has been transformed. The farmers have built good houses and have put large areas of land under cultivation. Life stock development has received a tremendous impetus and the introduction of modern sanitary equipment on New Zealand farms is now almost universal.

◆

In Canada we have made spasmodic efforts to deal with this problem. The Province of British Columbia has provided very advanced legislation on the subject of long-term credits. Unfortunately, the war situation has had an adverse effect on the working-out of the scheme. The Province of Manitoba has also made a notable contribution to the subject and has loaned some $2,000,000 under their Act. The Province of Alberta has likewise provided legislation, which it is now rumoured is being recast and improved. All this, however, is merely begging the question. What is required is a thorough Federal investigation of the whole subject, not so much with reference to the rural credit systems of other countries, but with a very complete understanding of the particular problems that confront us in the Dominion of Canada. Legislation in this matter should then be passed by the Federal Government, based on co-operative effort with the Provinces. It is clear that the Dominion Government can borrow more advantageously in the world's market than the Provinces, which would mean cheaper money to the farmer without any additional expense to anyone. The whole subject should be dealt with in a statesmanlike manner and with a clear comprehension of its tremendous importance to the agricultural advancement of Canada.

SIXTEEN

The Man on the Land

I WISH I HAD the power to impress the reader profoundly with the all-important idea that successful agriculture is the only sound foundation upon which a newer and better Canada may, in course of time, be built. I do not wish to assert that agriculture is the foundation of the wealth and greatness of all countries, although many students of political economy adhere to this belief and I could perhaps myself produce reasonable arguments in support thereof. It is sufficient for my purposes if I can make it clear that it is so, at least, as far as Canada is concerned.

The agricultural resources of Canada defy, in point of potential wealth, all effort of imagination or comprehension. This statement is literally true. Our present agricultural production is a mere drop in the proverbial bucket, in comparison with our future possibilities. The value of United States farms, equipment and stock is roughly 50 billions of dollars. The farmers of that country sold annually prior to the war, dairy products to the value of some 600 millions; poultry products, 250 millions; wool, 66 millions; domestic animals, 1,600 millions, and farm crops, six billions. The total of these items alone runs into eight and a half billions.

The table on page 160 shows Canada's agricultural production for the years 1915 to 1917.

Prior to the war Canada's total industrial production, including all the products of our mines and forests, was approximately a bil-

CANADA'S AGRICULTURAL PRODUCTION

	1915	1916	1917
Field crops	$825,371,000	$886,495,000	$1,144,637,000
Farm animals:			
Horses exported	1,842,000	4,701,00	4,385,000
Beef cattle, 20 p.c. of estimated total value	30,500,000	41,300,000	54,119,000
Sheep, 20 p.c. of estimated total value	3,262,000	4,200,000	7,115,000
Swine: Number, plus 16 p.c. for animals born and slaughtered within the year, 125 lb. meat per animal (1915, 8½ cents per lb.; 1916, 12 cents per lb.; 1917, 17.33 cents per lb.)	38,354,000	60,000,000	90,950,000
Wool: 12 million lbs., 28 cents, 1915; 37 cents, 1916; 59 cents, 1917	3,366,000	4,440,000	7,000,000
Factory cheese and creamery butter	51,482,000	62,479,000	74,487,000
Dairy butter: Quantity estimated on basis of Census, 1911; price, 25 cents per lb. in 1915; 27 cents per lb. in 1916; 30 cents per lb. in 1917	45,000,000	47,000,000	103,072,000
Home-made cheese: Quantity estimated on basis of Census of 1911; price, 15 cents per lb. in 1915; 18 cents per lb. in 1916.	278,000	351,000	263,000
Whole milk: Quantity estimated in Census Report of August 23, 1917; price at 6 cents per quart, 1915 and 1916; 7.5 cents per quart, 1917	49,245,000	42,986,000	55,000,000
Fruits and vegetables, say	35,000,000	35,000,000	40,000,000
Poultry and eggs, say	35,000,000	35,000,000	40,000,000
Gross total value	$1,118,694,000	$1,223,952,000	$1,621,028,000

lion dollars. Study the above record of what agriculture has done, draw the comparison between industrial and agricultural production, then take a swift look at the future and realize the significance of this fact: In the three prairie provinces alone, Canada has an agricultural area greater than one half of the total agricultural area of the entire United States!

Try to visualize what it all means—what stupendous potential wealth lies dormant in those black acres west of Lake Superior. Remember, too, that this land has scarcely any equal in point of productiveness and lasting qualities. How small Canada's vast war-debt looks, beside a season's possible production of this area! And do not lose sight of what all this ultimately means to the industrial development of Canada, if the goose that lays the golden egg is not killed by misguided efforts.

We must bend our energies to making Canada prosperous along the path that nature has so clearly indicated. We must all get down to bed-rock and think in terms of agriculture.

◆

It is well for a virgin country to take stock of itself in good time. Nations, like individuals, must select their occupations. The question must be answered: "What are you going to be?" Your statesmen must answer for you and determine whether your desires can be realized, and put you in the way of attaining your ambition. Canada now is at the parting of the ways. What is our leading industry going to be? This must be determined, once and for all time.

Switzerland and Italy are frankly concerned chiefly with attracting tourist traffic. They are the great holiday countries of Europe. The legislation and administration of these countries is shaped to attract well-to-do people, on pleasure bent. On the other hand, Denmark, Holland, New Zealand, Australia and many other countries similarly situated realize that agriculture and live stock production must always be their chief industries. No stone is left unturned to promote, in every legitimate way, the admitted primary industry.

Canada's ideal might well be to promote a happy and contented agricultural population, even at the sacrifice of certain more or less artificial industries which we have been endeavouring to nurse into active and profitable existence, ever since the days of Confederation. Let us ask ourselves in all seriousness whether it is worth while to run the risk of strangling our agriculture for the sake of these industrial weaklings adopted by the State. Let us rest absolutely assured that we cannot have it both ways. If the farmer is to be deprived of his best markets and has to divert his hard-earned profits to subsidize industry, he cannot prosper. We must make our choice.

◆

Just as a mere matter of interesting speculation, does it not seem paradoxical that Canada, which has been so abundantly blessed with agricultural wealth, should deliberately set about to create in this fresh new country the very conditions from which the European has fled in terror and disgust? Are we to conclude that there can be no human happiness without unsightly chimneys, belching forth their poisonous smoke? Do we enjoy the spectacle of streams of pale, toilworn humanity, wending their weary way into the slums and tenements apparently inseparable from this much vaunted industrial development? Is it worth the price of destroyed agriculture? Have we become such abject worshippers of the golden calf that we are ready to sacrifice everything that makes nations sound and great? Other countries have found it possible to become reasonably prosperous and contented on a basis of agricultural production. Such industries as naturally come into existence wherever agriculture is prosperous will automatically follow.

Fifty-six per cent of Canada's population makes its living directly from the soil. A large percentage of the production of the other basic industries, mining, lumbering and fishing, is also absorbed by the farm. Out of the total value of our manufactured articles in 1915, a fairly normal year, less than one-third went into our external trade. Half a million people found employment in these industries. Four million people lived directly off the farm. Heaven only knows how many indirectly gained their livelihood off this enormously preponderating section of the community. It is surely well within the mark to assert that at least 90 per cent of the population of Canada, be they engaged in trade, industry, transportation or in any other line of human endeavour, depend absolutely on our agriculture for their daily bread and the prosperity of their undertakings.

I want to make it clear that Canada's prosperity depends entirely on a prosperous agricultural population. Consequently, sacrifices can safely be made by the general community to assist agriculture, while undue burdens on agriculture should not be tolerated for a moment. These are points which our public men must keep constantly in mind. Without these guiding principles in administration, Canada will remain in her present rut.

In Canada, as elsewhere, the really influential citizen lives in town. In Canada, as elsewhere, the most appalling ignorance of rural affairs prevails amongst our urbanites. Once these good people could be brought to understand and sympathize with the man on the land, a new era would dawn. The education of our urban dweller, therefore, I regard as one of our great problems, requiring urgent attention.

———————◆———————

Just prior to the war we had a striking object lesson in Canada upon the economic effect of a languishing agriculture. It apparently created no lasting impression upon the public mind. In 1914 Canada was, beyond all doubt, drifting with the tide towards a veritable precipice. A widespread financial panic was impending, which might have swept into oblivion many financial, industrial and commercial enterprises in Eastern Canada. It would, like an avalanche, have gathered greater and greater force on its destructive path. Who can say where it would have ended?

Almost at the psychological moment, the great European war broke out and to it was conveniently attributed the gathering clouds on the domestic horizon. Our captain of industry or financial magnate, when in confidential mood, will now readily admit that the war was only a contributory cause, which, however, in the end became our financial salvation. Exigencies of war enabled us promptly to do many high-handed things to save the situation which otherwise could never have been justified, such as declaring general moratoria, facilitating drastic retrenchments, absorbing surplus workers in our military forces and adopting many other extraordinary heroic remedies to save us from the soup kitchen and widespread liquidation and insolvency. Then came the turn of the tide ushering in war orders, high prices, increased agricultural and industrial production and rapidly mounting exports. In a twinkling almost, we sailed into the smooth waters of sleek, opulent prosperity.

What were the causes that had brought Canada to the very brink of panic in 1914? It is of national importance that we should dissect and locate them, although I am aware that we do not talk about these unpleasant matters in polite society nowadays. The recollection of what might have been is a grotesque nightmare which we would fain consign to the inner-most recesses of our memory. It has a lesson of vast significance for Canada. It would assuredly tell us, if it could, that a multitude of our Canadian business houses and industries were tottering drunkenly in 1914 owing to the simple and sordid fact that they could not collect their outstanding accounts in Western Canada because, speaking generally and vulgarly, the Western farmer was "dead broke" and could not, therefore, pay his bills amounting in the aggregate to many millions of dollars. World prices of his products had been depressed for some considerable time and, to cap the climax, he had had a succession of disastrous crops.

Homesteaders who were able to do so had abandoned their farms or were getting ready to give up the fight. Immigration had ceased in sympathy with the unfavourable agricultural prospects. Farming was on "the toboggan." New settlers who had purchased land could not meet their deferred payments. The crazy townsite, land, oil and other "booms," nourished largely on outside capital and engineered by outside gamblers, had collapsed ingloriously. Centres of population and the more recently settled farming districts were becoming depopulated and almost every emigrant left undischarged liabilities behind him. Western towns and cities were making frantic efforts to stave off receiverships at the instance of bondholders, and our banks were becoming decidedly nervous and were calling in loans wholesale. It is a ghastly retrospect, but now, at the height of our prosperity, is an appropriate moment to remember it all. Then came the outbreak of the war, a bumper crop in 1915, high prices for wheat and live stock—and the West was off again on the high road of prosperity carrying industrial Canada along!

The Canadian farmer has now enjoyed a few years of prosperity and has been able to discharge his debts—which he always does when he can. He is able to buy more freely and eastern industry and business, consequently, are flourishing. It is curious how persistently our minds are focussed upon the present to the utter exclusion of the unpleasant past and all its lessons. We were, presumably, functioning under normal conditions in Canada until 1915. We have been, and probably shall be, functioning abnormally from that time until about 1920, when we may expect to become normal again. We have seen what "normal" meant up to 1915. Are we going to court a repetition of such a state of affairs? Or will the majority of our leading men frankly acknowledge that in the light of past events, there can be no prosperity in Canada that does not have its genesis in the soil of our country? Shall we cease sneering at the farmer when he gives expression to his well-founded anxiety about the uncertain future, and perhaps makes reconstruction proposals that may not appear strictly orthodox? Rest assured that the situation does not call for supercilious criticism or offensive imputations. Every thoughtful and patriotic citizen, irrespective of trade, profession or political affiliation, will be well advised to study the real difficulties confronting this country and to contribute his quota towards the solution of the many vital problems that surround agriculture, in the east as well as in the west.

We cannot, of course, control wind and weather and ensure favourable crop conditions. That is in other hands. But we can, if we will, do much to ensure that when the farmer has anything to sell he shall get it to market in good condition and at reasonable cost, that profitable markets shall not be artificially closed to him, that, in fact, the returns from his business shall be such that he can survive the lean years and thus keep the wheel of industry moving steadily to the everlasting advantage of everyone who calls Canada his home. It is not a class question. It is our one, great national problem. We might easily have had four to five million people west of Lake Superior by this time, with a corresponding industrial development east of the Great Lakes. They are not there because, since Confederation, we have administered that western empire as a great Canadian estate under absentee ownership. We have had majority rule in Canada with a vengeance!

◆

Agriculture may well be termed "the great gamble." The farmer's occupation involves a life of unremitting toil. He must compete in the open markets of the world with farmers of other countries and climates—the black, the brown, the yellow and the white races who have been working at high pressure for centuries and will probably go on doing so for many more generations. Take it one year with another, our farmer makes a fair living and nothing more. And, besides, he has considerable capital invested in his business, on which he draws only a very moderate return. He is at the mercy of the capriciousness of the seasons. Nothing he can do will enable him altogether to forecast results. Neither can he fix the values of his products. If the season is good in Russia or the Argentine or India, the Canadian farmer must sell his wheat at a discount. The cost of producing it does not enter into the calculation at all. He comes into the game, but other people play the cards.

I strongly entertain the opinion that there are many, many small farmers in Canada today, who would gladly exchange their present uncertain occupation for that of the railway man or other unionized employee, with his short and regular hours, his certain pay, absence of business worry, and freedom from that continual pressure for further capital investment, which absorbs every hard earned cent the farmer contrives to set aside in good years, and makes his life a burden in bad ones. The demands of his business for more and more capital investment also effectually prevent his enjoying the ordinary modern improvements and home comforts that almost every town-dweller would consider absolute essentials in life. If the farmer is doubtful on this point, just ask his wife. She has studied the deadly parallel and appreciates the differences between her daily life and that of her sister in town, as far as physical ease, comforts and recreations are concerned.

The farmer is the willing, sweating beast of burden of modern society. Politically, he is a nonentity. He has scarcely yet learned the art of team work. Socially, the town dweller is inclined to regard him as inferior. Economically, he foots the bill for the whole nation. He is the foundation, everybody admits, and like the literal foundation, he carries the entire dead-weight of the whole structure. He is the national paymaster-general. Men and masters in the cities may fight and squabble over pay and over hours and over principles, but when the settlement is finally made, it is the farmer, the greatest ultimate consumer of manufactured goods and of transportation, who foots the bill, because he cannot pass the burden on to any one else.

◆

The high cost of living is a safe topic of conversation these days. It holds everybody's interest and attention. As usual, Farmer Hodge bears the brunt of the criticism. How frequently one hears an argument end with the profound observation: "The farmers must all be getting wealthy." A standard weekly household budget has been worked out by the Dominion Department of Labour in connection with cost of living investigations. In the last month of the year 1918 the weekly average amounted to approximately $26.35 for a family of five. This cost was distributed as follows: Rent, $4.85; Clothing, $4.90; Fuel and lighting, $3.06; Meat and meat products, $4.24; Bread and flour, $1.87; Groceries, $3.10, and Produce generally supplied direct from the farm, $4.33. We might safely add another $5.00 for drugs, doctor and miscellaneous expenses, which would run the budget over $30 out of which the farmer receives directly a maximum of $4.33 and, indirectly, a mere fraction of the meat and bread expenditure. Our city consumers should study this statement and revise their views.

But is the farmer getting wealthy? He is undoubtedly much better off than he was some years ago, by reason of higher prices for his products, which are not quite offset by higher cost of labour and of general operations, which constitute a very considerable item. But it is important that the layman shall understand the situation. Professor Leitch recently made a farm survey of Oxford County, Ontario. He assumes this area to be fairly representative of the province. He found that 450 Oxford dairy-farmers, investigated by him earned on an average, a little below $1,200 per annum as a result of about 13 hours work per day for seven days a week, and also including the work of their wives and younger children. These figures are absolutely vouched for and are based on painstaking inquiry on the ground. So much for Eastern Canada.

As far as the West is concerned, I fortunately have actual figures from one of our large Western farms, of which I am part owner and, therefore, can vouch for the correctness of my information. Very exact cost records have been kept in connection with this enterprise ever since its inception. We operate on 4,000 acres and have been in business since 1912. Our gross operating cost increased from $14,252 in 1913 to $31,572 in 1917 on practically the same area. We produced about 39,000 bushels of wheat in the former year at a cost of 37 cents a bushel and, under the same management, 42,000 bushels in 1917 at a cost of 83 cents a bushel. In 1918 owing to crop failure the cost was, of course, abnormal and a fair comparison cannot, therefore, be established. For the benefit of those who are interested, I may mention that in 1918 our expenses were $22,000 for which we practically received no return whatever. Our operating practice is very similar to that of the average farm and may be accepted as a fair indication of the volume of increase in general cost of farm operation in Western Canada.

There is, however, another aspect of the cost of living grievance worthy of serious consideration. The late J.J. Hill summed the case up as the "cost of high living." He was a famous coiner of

epigrams. The town consumer now is bemoaning his fate and looking longingly back to the days when a hundred dollars a month was
equivalent to decent comfort. That period may fitly be catalogued
as the days of the "high cost of low living!" Canada has paid an extravagant price in postponed and arrested national development for
the halcyon days of ten cent eggs and butter, twelve cent poultry,
fifty cent wheat and apples at a dollar a barrel, all of which spelled
white slavery on the farm, unmitigated serfdom. With prematurely
broken-down men and women, who never knew what recreation,
decent comfort and household conveniences meant. We paid the
price also in farms abandoned by the old people, in utter despair,
following the rush cityward of all the young farm men and women,
who wisely concluded that the worst the city had to offer in the way
of drudgery, low pay and indifferent living surroundings, was
vastly superior almost to the best the farm could do for them. Even
under those wretched conditions, some farmers made money. One
is never permitted to forget that! But it was generally accomplished
by practising abject penury, which made the farmer of that day a
by-word, and at a cost in sweat and blood that the present generation would scorn to emulate. And it is well they should.

I strongly entertain the hope that happier days are now in store
for the man on the land. He has of late years received a reward for
his work that will presently enable him to put more brains and less
brawn into his effort. He will be able to enjoy the comforts of modern conveniences in his home and an occasional holiday. The moderate price motor-car and the rural telephone are banishing isolation. His social standing will be improved and the farm will offer
sufficient inducements to the young people to anchor them to rural
life. In fact, everything points to the regeneration of agriculture.
These improved conditions will finally be reflected in the industrial
life of the nation. The farmer will be a better customer for manufactured products than hitherto, and Canada will gradually approach
a much sounder and more normal industrial development than we
have enjoyed up to the present.

Decidedly, Canada cannot afford to pay much less for agricultural products than the present scale. Let us level up to that rather than attempt to reduce it. Let us also study and simplify our intricate and expensive system of distribution, so that the farmers' produce will reach the consumer without the intervention of many unnecessary middlemen. There, in my judgment, lies the chief and legitimate grievance of the consumer today. But the consumer is himself responsible for the higher cost of many food products. The general demand for highly refined package goods, whose intrinsic food value in comparison to price is absurdly small and whose popularity rests on nothing more substantial than striking labels, expensive containers and forced publicity, is a fruitful source of unprofitable expense; also the abuse of retail delivery and of credit, the outgrowths of our modern "house-keeping-by-telephone" system. Let us not wish it all on the farmer!

◆

I realize I have drawn a pretty dismal-looking picture of the farmers' life, and my intimate friends will smile incredulously, having in mind my own successful agricultural enterprises. These, however, are conducted on a large scale and backed by ample capital and are not in any way representative of average farming. I refer here to the ordinary small farmer in the East and to the man who loads his wife and babies and household goods on a wagon and goes out on the prairie to battle against nature. There are, however, compensations. The farmer makes wealth for himself and the State without levying toll on his fellow-man. His is altogether a beneficial and humane occupation, a blessing to all, a curse to none. He works in partnership with God Almighty and, if he does not prosper in the worldly sense as greatly as men in other occupations, his compensating advantages lie in the simple, healthful and independent life. With the great poet, Longfellow, we may well say:

> Happy he whom neither wealth nor fashion
> Nor the march of the encroaching city
>   Drives an exile
> From the hearth of his ancestral homestead.

No nation can attain greatness, nor remain great, without a steady influx into the hives of commerce and industry of the red blood from the farm. The national importance of promoting a prosperous rural life cannot be overestimated. Sir H. Rider Haggard says, on this subject:

> . . . . I will go further, and repeat what I have said before in other books—for it is one of the great objects of my life to advance this truth for the consideration of my fellow-countrymen—that the retention of the people on the land should be the great, and even the main, endeavour of the Western nations. Nothing can make up for the loss of them—no wealth, no splendour, no 'foreign investments,' no temporary success or glories of any kind. At any sacrifice, at any cost, all wise statesmen should labour to attain this end. The flocking of the land-born to the cities is the writing on the wall of our civilizations. This I have seen clearly for many years, and if I needed further evidence of its truth, I found it in plenty during my recent researches into the social work of the Salvation Army, which brought me into contact with thousands of waste mankind—the human refuse of the towns.
>
> Speaking generally, in the villages such folk scarcely exist. But in the cities, whither so many flock in faith and hope, they are manufactured by the hundred. For most of these the competition is too fierce. They are incompetent to cope with the difficulties of what is called high civilization. At the first touch of misfortune, of temptation, of sickness, they go down, and but too often fall, like Lucifer, to rise no more. The shelters, the jails, the hospitals, the workhouses, the Poor Law returns, all tell the same story. Moreover, what class of people are bred in the slums of Glasgow or of London? Yes, in Glasgow, where I was informed not long ago that one out of every twelve of the inhabitants has no home, but sleeps at night in some refuge or common lodging-house. . . .

There has been in Canada a noticeable tendency on the part of our rural people to flock to the towns and cities. In 1901, according to census figures, 37½% of our population lived in the towns. Ten years afterwards the proportion was 45½%. This is not a healthy development, but the cause is perfectly clear. Agriculture has, as previously stated, not been sufficiently attractive. There has not been enough profit in it and the present conditions of farm life will not stand comparison with town life. That is the case in a nutshell. Our young people know it and have left the farm.

◆

I can picture in my mind's eye our successful business-man, ponderously rising to his feet, deep indignation stamped upon his features. He is about to reiterate the conventional arguments [slamming] roundly our slovenly farming, the implements un-protected against wind and weather, the burning of strawstacks, the persistent production of cereals to the detriment of animal production and so on and so forth *ad nauseam*.

I have often thought that it is a most extraordinary thing that a man of business will, with the utmost sang-froid, criticize farm management and policy, when he would stand aghast if his hayseed brother assumed a similar attitude with regard to his business. Everybody welcomes an intelligent interest in rural affairs on the part of our town people. That is what I am pleading for. But it must not be dictatorial, nor must it assume, as a starting point, that all farmers are fools. There is no business or art practised anywhere re-quiring wider technical skill and knowledge. The farmer is part cap-italist, part manager, part mechanic, part scientist and part labourer. He cannot be expected to know it all, from browbeating a stupid or timid bank manager to exercising the function of midwife to the cow with the crumpled horn. Let us be tolerant.

◆

We are asked here why our Western farmer grows so much wheat to the exclusion of other products, notably those of the dairy. The explanation is perfectly simple to those who understand. He is merely following the line of least resistance as we all do. Wheat pays fairly well, comparatively speaking, on our new lands. It involves less hand labour than other branches of farming, because a greater proportion of the work is mechanical. Grain is essentially, naturally, and logically, the first crop of new land and gives the quickest return. It takes less capital to produce than any other crop. Several other reasons could be given, but one more is perhaps sufficient, and it is this: the mere fact that wheat is being so largely produced is fairly good evidence that it pays better than other crops in our present state of national development. This should be wholly convincing, unless we are to accept the theory that our wheat growers are lunatics or wholly incompetent, which is hardly safe.

Besides, with the present scarcity of competent labour, who would undertake the heavy responsibilities of the dairy farm either in the West or in the East? Men simply will not work the long hours,—Saturdays, Sundays, holidays—incidental to this branch of farming, as long as they can get work, at the same pay, with Union hours, in the towns. Can you blame them? In the end, the farmer's wife has to take over the job, and trudge to the cow-stable in the slush and snow, bucket in hand, and milk cows by the light of a lantern, morning and night. When you pay 75¢ a pound for butter, you dainty, pink and white, altogether charming city women, think of that!

———————◆———————

Compare the lot of agricultural labour in Canada with the organized labour of the cities and what do we find?

The hod carrier appears at his job at 8 A.M. and works until 5 P.M. with an hour off at noon. On Saturday he quits at noon and has a rest period until Monday morning. His home, however humble it may be, has the usual modern conveniences. He is able to associate with his fellows and enjoy all the attractions of the city, including the movies. His wages are generally adequate to the extent of enabling him to live and dress decently. His organization sees to that.

The farmhand rises from his slumbers at 5 A.M. and does his chores. He has his breakfast at 6:30. His team goes out to work at 7 A.M.; more chores at noon; steady work until 6 P.M.; then supper and more chores. When the day ends he has probably worked from 14 to 16 hours. He frequently sleeps in a loft. He has very inadequate facilities for keeping himself clean and in a great many instances he lives in a mess that his city brother would not put up with for a minute. He tumbles to bed, dead tired, when the day's work is done. By comparison, it is the life of a serf. No recreation, no time for self-improvement, whilst his wages are probably much inferior to what the city labourer is able to command.

To argue that competent farm labour is not entitled to the same remuneration as a hod carrier, is the rankest kind of nonsense. A competent farm hand, able to look properly after live stock and do ordinary farm work, is a much more skilled man than even the carpenter or bricklayer receiving five to seven dollars a day. How long will these conditions prevail? When will the agricultural labourer demand, first, equal wages with city labour and, secondly, a bonus to compensate him for his isolation and inferior living conditions? And when that time comes, what will the Canadian farmer do? In his present circumstances, he cannot meet those demands and live. He cannot pass the burden on to the consumer.

◆

I notice in the press a message to the farmers of Canada from the Rt. Hon. Mr. Protero, for whose judgment I have tremendous respect. It is to the effect that we should develop our chilled meat trade. This, of course, involves the finishing in Canada of our beef and mutton, which we should be able to do more cheaply than it could be done in Great Britain. We must hope for better things, but in the past, it has not perhaps been a particularly attractive business.

The profits in live stock feeding may be divided into the direct and indirect. The indirect returns are obvious. The farmer gets the manure to keep up the fertility of the land. By feeding them at home, he saves hauling his various field crops to market. He is able to employ labour all the year round instead of only for the summer season. Cattle feeding in Great Britain is practically down to a basis where the feeder only expects to get a fair price for the feeding materials raised on his farm, and his money back for those he has actually purchased, and to take his profits out entirely in the shape of indirect returns, principally, of course, the manure. Even in the United States, east of the Mississippi River, the feeding industry is very frequently conducted on a similar basis. Where hogs follow steers, their market value may represent a by-product profit. I have often wondered how our Canadian manufacturers would like to conduct business on such a margin? Fancy, asking them to take their sole profit in the shavings and iron filings of the shop!

In any other line of manufacture or production of any sort, it is a commonly accepted axiom that the performance of each operation required to bring any commodity to its finished state, is properly rewarded according to the amount of outlay, time and skill involved. Not so in live stock feeding, however. The cost of raw material, labour and value of the finished product bear no necessary relation to each other whatever. As usual, the farmer has to be the gambler and bear all risk. No business man would entertain a proposition like that, for a minute. The gamble frequently is, as to whether or not he gets his money back as well as his indirect profit. And then he has to run the risk of disease, accident and fluctuating markets.

It is freely stated amongst cattle feeders in the U.S. that if they have many more years like 1914 and 1915, the cattle-feeder will be looking about for someone to feed him!

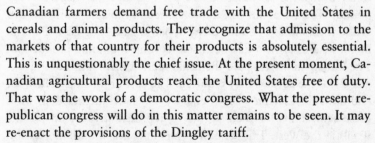

Canadian farmers demand free trade with the United States in cereals and animal products. They recognize that admission to the markets of that country for their products is absolutely essential. This is unquestionably the chief issue. At the present moment, Canadian agricultural products reach the United States free of duty. That was the work of a democratic congress. What the present republican congress will do in this matter remains to be seen. It may re-enact the provisions of the Dingley tariff.

Otherwise well-informed people often wonder why our West has been so slow in developing. Those who have personally assisted in this disappointing process entertain no illusions on that subject. It is clear as daylight. Until the Dingley tariff was repealed a few years ago, practically every head of cattle, sheep or hog, every fleece of wool, every hide, in fact, every animal product of the West was handicapped in seeking an outside market. The price realized on every item of such products was precisely twenty-seven and a half per cent less than its proper selling price. Or, to put the case another way, the market value was fixed in Chicago and it cost us 27½ per cent to get in there. The market in Canada was based on the Chicago price, less the duty.

On the other hand, on every tool and implement the Western farmer bought, and on his clothing, boots and various other items entering into his daily living and work, he had to pay about the same amount of duty, directly or indirectly. He was penalized coming and going.

So we find that John Smith, farmer or rancher, who, in the days of the Dingley tariff, ranged his live stock in the Sweet Grass Hills, just north of the International Boundary in Alberta, sold his $50 steer for approximately $36.25, while John Jones, who ranged his cattle a mile or so away, but south of the magical line, was able to get the full value. And in addition the fortunate Jones was able to purchase his haying machinery at 15 per cent to 20 per cent less than his Canadian neighbour. Is it any wonder that agricultural development was slow in Western Canada?

For years I had wool to sell in the West. The same wool that today brings the flockmaster 68¢ per pound, I have sold at 7¢ a pound! We have about two million sheep in Canada. Our total clip is about 12 million pounds of wool per annum. The Canadian demand is, and always has been, far beyond the home production. The Canadian buyers paid the usual market price in Bradford, England, for the surplus they required. The cost of the imported wool laid down in Canada was, of course, very much higher than what these same mills, or their agents or representatives, paid for the wools in the West. This state of affairs only lasted until the Wilson tariff law went into effect and we were given free admission for our wool into the United States. This at once improved the situation from the Western standpoint, for with the U.S. buyer in the field the Canadian market was not the only one available and our wools advanced 27½ per cent at once. This criminal attitude of the Canadian mill owners apparently brought its own punishment in the end. They made the blunder of depressing prices far below what "the traffic would bear." Hence our depleted sheep stocks today, all over Canada, and Canadian mills are now forced to pay a premium for foreign wool.

I cannot resist introducing a personal experience, which tells the story better than statistics. The year before the Dingley tariff was repealed and while Canadian wool growers were still compelled to sell at the prices dictated by a small group of protected pirates, my concern had a clip of 50,000 lbs. of wool to dispose of. We decided we would not be held up. We sent to New South Wales for a wool press and bales, secured the services of a New Zealand wool sorter and classifier, erected a very primitive wool scouring plant on our property, hand-scoured our wool and turned it out according to the best Australian traditions and shipped it to the London market.

I went to England and saw the shipment sold. It created some sensation and realized within a fraction of the highest price reached at the September sales, in competition with wool from every country in the world. Our Canadian buyers that year had the satisfaction of finally paying the full price and probably bringing this wool back across the Atlantic into the bargain. We actually did better, after paying all these unusual expenses, than had we accepted the best offer at home. These are the problems the Canadian farmer has had to face and solve—if he could. He hates tariffs and with good reason.

◆

Present market conditions for animal products are, of course, quite satisfactory to the farmer. The repeal of the Dingley tariff opened up the United States market barely in time to save our West. Then came the war and war-prices. The latter situation is obviously an abnormal development. It is not, by any means, safe to settle down to the comfortable conviction that we shall have unhampered entry into the United States for our agricultural products forever. As is the case in all protected countries, the tariff south of the line is simply a political football. With the republican party in power in the United States again, the pressure to restore the tariff on agricultural products there is going to be very strong. I should not care to predict the effect west of Lake Superior, should such an eventuality occur. It might shake Canadian Confederation to its very foundation.

SEVENTEEN

The Returned Soldier and Matters Military

CANADA'S DEBT TO the men who went overseas to take part in the great crusade against autocracy, can never be adequately expressed in terms of mere dollars and cents, which means—that no Government can satisfactorily liquidate Canada's moral liability by act of Parliament. It reduces itself to an obligation between man and man. It becomes, in the truest sense, a debt of honour by the man who stayed behind to the man who bravely embarked upon the great crusade. This conception of the case every patriotic employer in Canada must have engraved indelibly upon his mind. He—personally, individually—is responsible for the welfare of one or more of those who are returning without any definite prospect of employment. With a general and complete realisation of this obligation on the part of Canadian employers, the re-establishment problem solves itself.

But the returned soldier also has grave responsibilities resting upon him. He went "over there" as a sacred duty. He did not offer his body and soul for sale for a paltry dollar-and-ten a day and the prospect of a pension if disabled. He now represents all that is finest and best and noblest in our national life. It is for the rest of us to endeavour to live up to his standard in the future. We look to him for example and guidance. He has wandered through the valley of the shadow of death and has unconsciously imbibed wisdom, tolerance and higher aims from the very source of the fountain of life. Canada feels that in this period of widespread social stress and turmoil she may safely depend upon her "boys" to exert a steadying influence on the more unstable and less responsible elements in her population and that she may confidently anticipate their loyal and public-spirited assistance in the process of rearing—perhaps all too slowly and laboriously for many of us—a democracy for which no citizen need blush.

———————◆———————

The Dominion Government, with commendable promptness, made provision early in the war, for a scheme of soldiers' settlement and later appointed a small commission to work out details. The broad features of the scheme were outlined in the Soldiers' Settlement Act. Briefly, the intending military settler looks over the country and selects a homestead or a parcel of land for purchase. He is then advanced a sum of money as a loan, at a fairly low rate of interest and repayable in twenty years. He doubtless fills in and signs many forms, receives the blessings of a paternal Government or Board and then embarks on the great adventure. To the unsophisticated this plan will doubtless look very attractive at first sight. It relieves the Government of a tremendous amount of administration and responsibility. The settler is absolutely on his individual resources and the paternal atmosphere is absent.

———————◆———————

The experience of Western Canada, broadly speaking, has been that the first settler on the land has rarely succeeded. The permanent and successful occupant has generally been the second and sometimes even the third. The problem of creating new capital, while taking care of a family and paying interest charges on borrowed money, is a task involving such a degree of frugality, capacity and unremitting labour that only comparatively few men measure up to the standard. In this respect, farming is, of course, in no way different from any other class of business.

In approaching the subject of assisted settlement of soldiers, it behooves the Government to walk warily. There is little or no precedent in Canada as a guide. In some of the Australian States, similar effort has been made along lines of general colonization. The United States reclamation service has also approached something of the sort in the disposal of irrigated lands. The only fairly analogous cases in Canada are the few assisted colonization enterprises at Yorkton and Saltcoats, the early Mennonite settlement in Manitoba and the ready-made farm scheme of the Canadian Pacific Railway. The Mennonite colonization was eminently successful, but due entirely to the human element. The Yorkton and Saltcoats colonization projects, including Crofter colonization, were dismal failures. The C.P.R. ready-made farm scheme is the nearest approach to what the Government proposes to undertake, and even that differs in an essential point.

The Railway Company supplied the settler with land, improvements and seed grain. The settler was supposed to have capital of his own sufficient to stock the farm, purchase implements and carry himself and his family until revenue came in. In other words, he was only financed to the extent of 60 or 70 per cent of his capital. The returned soldier will in most cases have to be financed for his entire capital. It takes a very prosperous business indeed to enable a man to carry the same on, provide for necessary development, keep his family, pay interest on borrowed money, and also to repay the entire capital invested. . . .

◆

I shall waste very little time in criticizing the present plan for soldiers' settlement announced by the Government, if, indeed, this product of a simple and trusting mind should be dignified by referring to it as a "plan." While the Act does not specifically say so, it is perfectly obvious that it contemplates unorganized settlement, meaning that any soldier can take up Dominion lands or purchase lands anywhere and apply to the Board for a loan. To persist in such a course is to court inevitable disaster, from the point of view of administration and of the success of the individual settler. The Government apparently fears that, if gathered in colonies, the settlers would find it convenient and expedient to organize indignation meetings for the purpose of expressing criticisms of the Government and the administration. By continually comparing notes, grievances would be manufactured and agitators would proceed to air them. Quite probable. In fact, that would be almost certain to occur. And it would be very disturbing to the Government and to the Board. It would be an unmitigated nuisance. No one realizes more keenly than the writer the many objections to the settlement of people in colonies. He has "lived" with the problem! On the other hand, in spite of all the drawbacks and objections, it is my absolute judgment that colony settlement is, in this case, the only feasible plan—the only plan, in fact, that will have a ghost of a chance to succeed, to any large extent.

I enumerate below the principal objections to the present "plan" of settlement proposed by the Federal authorities:

(a) The Government will be absolutely unable to protect adequately the large advances made to settlers for investment in live stock and other liquid assets, and to promote the wise and profitable investment of this borrowed capital.

(b) Opportunities for effecting economy and efficiency through co-operative effort amongst the settlers themselves will not be present. While this in itself would not lead to failure, it will be a serious obstacle to that measure of success the country will expect.

(c) Special educational work amongst these settlers would be impossible or, at any rate, difficult and spasmodic.

(d) The character of this proposed scattered settlement would simply be reduced to, or might even fall below, the general average of prairie settlement; and the experience has been that less than 50 per cent of such settlers succeed. The Government cannot afford a 50 per cent failure.

(e) The Government must take into the most serious consideration the fact that every failure under any scattered or unorganized "Soldiers' Settlement" plan will involve part or total loss of a large part of its investment, as there will be no one to watch such investment from day to day and to step in and protect it in case of emergency or to give the settler a helping hand at a critical moment.

◆

The land problem is admittedly the cornerstone of any colonization plan. The progress of the best settled and richest districts of Western Canada has for years been retarded through the presence of enormous areas of undeveloped Indian Reserves. Some of these lands are amongst the very best in Western Canada.

I am informed that the total male Indian population between the ages of 16 and 65, living on Reserves in the three Prairie Provinces, is approximately, 5,000. The area of the various Reserves is approximately 3,000,000 acres. If each male Indian between the ages of 16 and 65 were settled upon a 320-acre farm, 1,600,000 acres would be absorbed. This would leave an area of 1,400,000 acres of the best lands in Western Canada available for Military Colonization. On a 200-acre unit plan this would provide for 7,000 soldiers. This would apparently go a long way towards solving the problem.

I am not unmindful of the serious obstacles in the way of dealing in such a manner with Indian Reserves. The fact remains, however, that under pressure of mere public opinion, it has been successfully done during recent years in several instances. The psychological moment has now apparently arrived for dealing, finally and completely, with the whole troublesome question. A crisis has arisen which justifies the Government in doing things autocratically, if necessary. The Government can do things today that it could not do before, and probably will never be able to do again.

An announcement that the Government proposed to deal finally with these Indian Reserves and in this manner would be hailed with delight by practically every resident in Western Canada. It would also seem most appropriate that the returned soldiers should be settled on what are unquestionably the very best vacant lands in the West. In the face of a national necessity, such as this, shallow sentiment or Indian obstinacy should not be permitted to influence the Government's action in this great welfare undertaking. The Indian can be handsomely compensated and will, in the end, be much bet-

ter off with his individual holding than roaming over enormous undeveloped areas of highly valuable lands, now needed urgently for
national purposes.

◆

An Order-in-Council has recently been passed materially increasing
our future military establishment and also providing more adequate
pay than hitherto. One of the justifications set forth is the necessity
that may exist of rendering military aid to the civil authorities in
suppressing riots, or disturbances. It seems a very wise and reasonable move. But we should now grasp the opportunity to improve our whole army scheme. The enlisted men should be educated to take their places in civil life, upon discharge, on a higher
plane than they could reach prior to enlistment. We should in addition to military instruction, formulate a scheme of general education and vocational training that would make the time-expired man
a more useful citizen than he was when he entered the military service. We should dwell less on the pension idea in attracting recruits,
than on the facilities offered for learning useful trades in the very
generous spare time allowance customary in military life. Such a
plan would not interfere with adequate military training and the
added expense would be trifling. We should also stand a much better chance of attracting young men of a higher calibre to the rank
and file of military service than we can otherwise hope for.

In line with such a development would be a general plan to make
our permanent military forces more useful to the country in time of
peace than in the past. We are now making provision for 5,000 men
and probably four to five hundred officers. Half of this strength will
probably be infantry. Why not learn a lesson in economy and efficiency from other countries? The United States Engineering Corps
performs valuable services to that country in connection with public works. For instance, all harbour and canal construction has been
in its very capable hands for many years. The proposal was also
made that the U.S. Reclamation service should be under the jurisdiction of the military forces. There is a distinct tendency in the
United States to widen the scope and responsibilities of its

Engineering Corps, partly owing to the creditable fact that in its whole history, covering the expenditure of many millions of dollars, it has the unique record of only one or two minor misappropriation scandals. It has stood conspicuously for honesty and efficiency of a very high order. In European countries the practice of utilizing military Engineering units for public works is also general.

There is surely something to learn from other progressive countries in this respect. Why not enlist at least two-thirds of our proposed military establishment as Engineers? They could render useful civil services and, at the same time, be equally as effective as infantry in case of emergency. There is all sorts of survey work to be done in this new country and will be for many years to come. Why not take a hand in this?

There is no particular merit in a military unit devoting its entire attention to drill and recreation. We shall have greater all-round efficiency if our enlisted men feel that most of their time is constructively employed. They will also make better citizens.

EIGHTEEN

Education and Sane Standards

IT IS NOT MY purpose to formulate any new "high brow" educational theory. I am not qualified to undertake such a task. But I do know by this time, wherein my own and my children's education woefully failed. In the modern school, we impart knowledge of a kind. We do not properly educate. I can only direct attention to the deficiency, as I see it, leaving the remedy to be discovered and applied by the professional educationist. To prove one's case, it should only be necessary to call attention to the criminally low salaries paid to Canadian teachers and also to the class of teachers such a system naturally attracts. The teaching profession in Canada is merely a convenient halting place on the road to other things. It must be clear that, from a financial standpoint, no sane young man or woman would deliberately fit himself or herself for teaching as a life profession under the conditions that prevail. The average annual salary for female teachers in Ontario is $626, the average in rural schools in Manitoba is $621. In Quebec the figure is $563 in Protestant, and $273 in Roman Catholic Schools. In New Brunswick salaries to female teachers vary from $271.79 to $500.60 per annum. Nova Scotia statistics are discreetly silent on the subject. But why pursue the matter further? The feeblest intellect must comprehend that the "key industry" of Canada, i.e. the education of the rising generation, is generally in the hands of mere casuals, who loiter on the way a year or two at the teacher's desk and then proceed to more congenial and remunerative fields.

Much fault may also be found with our facilities for technical education. Some years ago, a most valuable report was made on this subject by a commission composed of highly-qualified men. It now forms part of our dusty, mildewed public records. No action was ever taken by the authorities to give effect to the well considered recommendations of this commission. When everything is said, how very insignificant is the artificial aid Governments can give to industrial development by means of tariffs, compared with the influence on industry of the technically-educated craftsman and skilled mechanic, backed by efficient and economical shop management and a sane business policy. We are far behind our neighbours in the south and most other progressive countries in this respect. We should permit nothing to stand in the way of creating the widest possible facilities in Canada for technical education of a very high order. This is one of the real and pressing needs of Canadian industries today.

The fate of our rural educational system has largely been in the hands of the "hardshell" farmer, who would unconsciously measure a teacher's salary against what he pays his hired hands, except for such regulating influences as are brought to bear in the more enlightened provinces. The result of this penurious attitude on Canada's part has, of course, been that our higher class teachers have most frequently found it advisable to go south of the line, where their services have received more substantial recognition. Our schools presumably impart a certain amount of useful knowledge to our children in a very mechanical sort of way. But I am far more concerned with the other side of education. What are we doing to implant in the young mind ideas of lofty citizenship and unselfish patriotism; of courtesy and toleration; of sane healthy ambition? It is argued that the home is the place for instruction in these subjects. I totally disagree. I would sooner delegate these to the school and teach my children the three R's at home, if necessary. The school atmosphere lends itself vastly better to effective and impressive lessons dealing with the humanities of life and duties of citizenship, than the perfunctory and irregular instruction the average pupil would receive on such subjects in the average home. It is not my desire to urge that the parents should be relieved of all responsibility for the instruction of their children, but merely that the teaching of the higher citizenship should be developed in our schools.

◆

I would like to say a word on modern tendencies towards false standards in life. The responsibility of the State is not to make men wealthy, but to make them wise, to teach the children to scorn sordid ambition and to discriminate intelligently between what is important and what is unimportant. The desire to acquire mere wealth is essentially ignoble, apart from the fact that few men can ever completely satisfy such a diseased ambition. One standard of wealth having been attained, another looms up ahead. It is an unsatisfactory goal. The intellectual State honours its great poets and artists, the humanitarian State its wise legislators and administrators, the militant State its great sailors and soldiers. The commercial State is apt to honour only its captains of commerce and industry. History leaves little doubt on that point. It, therefore, behooves the State, through its educational system, to destroy utterly false standards and to set up true and noble ones. The patriotic press of the country should carry on the good work and frown down any attempt to bestow praise where undeserved. The press, indeed, has almost the greater responsibility of the two. It staggers one to realize that this great factor in the life and future of the nation is too often in wholly irresponsible hands, to the extent that each individual newspaper proprietor is absolutely a law unto himself as to whether his paper is to be a power for good or for evil in his community, apart from the fact that his faculty of discrimination is not infrequently faulty.

It is precisely this worship of false standards that is almost wholly responsible for the present social unrest, and the impatience of labour with palliatory measures of reform. In the eye of the worker the "Golden Calf" is the great desideratum in life. In the acquisition of wealth he anticipates the happy solution of all his problems. Wealth and happiness become synonymous terms. That is the sum total of all he has been taught. The captain of industry becomes his hero. The thinker, the artist, the scholar are almost beneath contempt—men who live in garrets and starve. The only true measure of the value of a man's services is the material compensation he receives. The parson is just tolerated, looked upon as a bit of a crank, receiving the proverbial pittance and raising a large family on nothing, cheerfully serving his Lord and Master. And a certain section of the press of the country plays up these false ideas to the very limit. The men whose comings and goings are most carefully recorded, whose opinions are so respectfully solicited on all subjects, the men whose pictures most frequently adorn the front pages of such papers, are, almost invariably, the prosperous men. When Governments accord public honours, how often to they come the way of the humbler, but greater citizen? It is wealth, or the faculty to acquire wealth, that is most frequently the subject of public applause and public recognition.

◆

Perhaps man was not intended to be happy and contented. Maybe the mainspring of all human progress lies in the inherent discontent, restlessness and unhappiness of the individual, driving him into the mad race for further material possessions and success, as moderns are now taught to interpret the word. It is perhaps his very striving after these evanescent, hollow and unsatisfying things that builds up nations. If so we are assuredly living in a glorified lunatic asylum. Labouring under the mental hallucination that certain things are essential to happiness, which, as a matter of fact, have nothing to do with that elusive state of mind, we are permitting ourselves to be relentlessly driven into striving for these things, only to find, when they are attained, that they utterly fail to satisfy. All our stress and effort, therefore, is wasted as far as any personal recompense is concerned. The State or community would seem to be the only beneficiary.

In so far as equipping the embryo citizen to enter the ruthless struggle of life is concerned, our modern school system is probably all that could be desired. As I have tried to show, its efforts in teaching morality, courtesy and a true appreciation of the duties and responsibilities of citizenship, are woefully deficient. We have banished religion from our schools. What have we substituted? If ever there was a time when the young should be taught something about the deeper things in life, and the futility of worshipping false gods, it is the present. I cannot refrain from quoting here an extract from Smiles—whose books might well be included in our public school curriculum—upon the "art of living," which so few of us have studied and begun to understand:

. . . . The art of living deserves a place among the fine arts. Like literature, it may be ranked with the humanities. It is the art of turning the means of living to the best account—of making the best of everything. It is the art of extracting from life its highest enjoyment, and, through it, of reaching its highest results.

To live happily, the exercise of no small degree of art is required. Like poetry and painting, the art of living comes chiefly by nature: but all can cultivate and develop it. It can be fostered by parents and teachers, and perfected by self-culture. Without intelligence it cannot exist.

Happiness is not, like a large and beautiful gem, so uncommon and rare that all search of it is vain, all efforts to obtain it hopeless; but it consists of a series of smaller and commoner gems, grouped and set together, forming a pleasing and graceful whole. Happiness consists in the enjoyment of little pleasures scattered along the common path of life, which, in the eager search for some great and exciting joy, we are apt to overlook.

The art of living is abundantly exemplified in actual life. Take two men of equal means, one of whom knows the art of living, and the other not. The one has the seeing eye and the intelligent mind. Nature is ever new to him, and full of beauty. He can live in the present, rehearse the past, or anticipate the glory of the future. With him life has a deep meaning, and requires the performance of duties which are satisfactory to his conscience and are, therefore, pleasurable. He proves himself, acts upon his age, helps to elevate the depressed classes, and is active in every good work. His hand is never tired, his mind is never weary. He goes through life joyfully, helping others to its enjoyment. Intelligence, ever expanding, gives him every day fresh insight into men and things. He lays down his life full of honour and blessing, and his greatest monument is the good deeds he has done and the beneficent example he has set before his fellow creatures. .... It is not wealth that gives the true zest to life, but reflection, appreciation, taste, culture. Above all, the seeing eye and the feeling heart are indispensable. With these, the humblest lot may be made blessed. Labour and toil may be associated with the highest thoughts and the purest tastes. The lot of labour may thus become elevated and ennobled.

My chief complaint lies in the callous attitude of the citizen towards the State. He recognises no responsibilities. If a certain tax is imposed, his main effort is directed towards evading it wholly or in part. His code of honour permits him to defraud his country, when he would scorn not dealing with his fellow citizen as an honourable man should. It is a most curious mental process that condones robbing the state, i.e., all one's fellow citizens, and condemns defrauding an individual citizen. What has our public school system done to correct this point of view?

In conclusion, I deliberately reiterate the statement that the foundation of all sound and orderly human progress is education. To vary the formula, it may be added that the development of a broad spirit of toleration and of patriotism is equally essential. Possibly the former breeds the latter. A popular writer recently bemoaned our "lost sense of right and wrong," as the greatest tragedy of the hour. Perhaps this is where our education towards saner standards should really begin! The main problem involved in any sweeping social or political reform is not so much to decide upon and draft the particular measure of reform, as to fit successfully the human unit into the proposed new order. In other words, the nation programme must of necessity always be limited to the ability of the majority of the citizens to live up to it. This is the great brake on social progress and the discouraging feature about social reorganization. The main responsibility of the statesman is to realize when the psychological moment has arrived—when the State can safely act.

A nation's process of education and training often takes weird forms. Misfortune, persecution and starvation—each has played its part as national schoolmaster. A terrible upheaval, such as the world has witnessed during the past few years, is perhaps the most effective school of social reform for the multitude. It has compelled nations to co-operate and has brought vividly before the citizen its object lessons of successful public control, forced upon reluctant governments in the emergency. These lessons will not be forgotten. Social reform advanced a century in one mighty bound. Perhaps herein lies the justification, or divine purpose, of Armageddon.